easy
entertaining

easy entertaining

simple recipes for every occasion

RYLAND
PETERS
& SMALL

LONDON NEW YORK

Designer **Sarah Fraser**
Editor **Sharon Ashman**
Production **Deborah Wehner**
Art Director **Gabriella Le Grazie**
Publishing Director **Alison Starling**

Index Hilary Bird

First published in the United States
in 2004.

This paperback edition published
in 2007
by Ryland Peters & Small, Inc.
519 Broadway, 5th Floor
New York, NY 10012
www.rylandpeters.com

10 9 8 7 6 5 4 3 2 1

Text © Celia Brooks Brown, Maxine
Clark, Linda Collister, Clare Ferguson,
Manisha Gambhir Harkins, Elsa
Petersen-Schepelern, Louise Pickford,
Ben Reed, Fiona Smith, Sonia
Stevenson, Fran Warde, Lesley Waters
and Ryland Peters & Small 2004, 2007
Design and photographs
© Ryland Peters & Small 2004, 2007

Printed in China

ISBN-13: 978 1 84597 491 6
ISBN-10: 1 84597 491 3

The hardcover edition is catologed
as follows:

Library of Congress Cataloging-in-
Publication Data

Easy entertaining : simple recipes for
every occasion / Celia Brooks
Brown ... [et al.].
    p. cm.
Includes index.
  ISBN 1-84172-574-9
  1. Quick and easy cookery. 2.
Entertaining. I. Brown, Celia Brooks.
  TX833.5.E2773 2004
  641.5'55--dc22
                    2003023418

Notes

All spoon measurements are level
unless otherwise specified.

Ovens should be preheated to the
specified temperature. If using a
convection oven, cooking times should
be reduced according to the
manufacturer's instructions.

Uncooked or partially cooked eggs
should not be served to the very
young, the very old or frail, or to
pregnant women.

Specialty Asian ingredients are
available in larger supermarkets and
Asian stores.

To sterilize preserving jars, wash them
in hot, soapy water and rinse in
boiling water. Place in a large
saucepan and then cover with hot
water. With the saucepan lid on, bring
the water to a boil and continue
boiling for 15 minutes. Turn off the
heat, then leave the jars in the hot
water until just before they are to be
filled. Sterilize the lids for 5 minutes,
by boiling, or according to the
manufacturer's instructions. Jars
should be filled and sealed while
they are still hot.

contents

introduction

Entertaining can take many forms but the most important thing to bear in mind is that everyone should enjoy themselves—and that includes you, the cook. Whether you are planning a summer garden party or a quiet lunch for a close friend, arranging a smart dinner party or a casual weekend brunch, this book has a huge selection of recipe suggestions to suit. Throughout, the emphasis is on "easy," but this in no way compromises the food you can cook, its taste, or the "wow" factor. Here you will find a full range of dishes from around the world that will inspire you to create wonderful meals for your guests using only the freshest and tastiest ingredients.

Each recipe is presented in easy-to-follow stages to make your time in the kitchen as simple and as stress-free as possible. You will soon find yourself delving enthusiastically into the book's different chapters to come up with menus to suit your own culinary gatherings and the tastes of your guests. You will be amazed at the way entertaining can play such a pleasurable part in your social life.

So, don't waste any more time. Invite some friends round now and get reading— there's entertaining to be done!

brunch

pancakes

A stack of fluffy, homemade pancakes in the morning will keep you and your guests fueled for hours. Make the batter before bedtime and leave it overnight in the refrigerator. In the morning, you'll have a brunch feast in minutes.

1½ cups all-purpose flour

2 teaspoons baking powder

1 teaspoon salt

3 tablespoons sugar

1 cup milk

2 eggs, lightly beaten

4 tablespoons unsalted butter, melted, plus extra for cooking

maple butter syrup

⅓ cup maple syrup

2 tablespoons unsalted butter

makes 8–12, serves 4

Sift the flour, baking powder, salt, and sugar into a bowl. Mix the milk, eggs, and the 4 tablespoons melted butter in a large pitcher, then add the flour mixture and mix quickly to make a batter (don't worry about lumps—they're good). Alternatively, make the batter in a bowl and transfer to a pitcher.

Heat a cast-iron skillet or flat-surfaced griddle until medium hot. Grease lightly with extra butter, then pour in the batter in batches to make your pancakes 3–4 inches in diameter. Cook for 1–2 minutes on the first side or until bubbles form on top of the pancakes and the underside is golden, then flip each one over and cook for 1 minute more. Keep the pancakes warm in a low oven while you cook the remaining batches.

Heat the maple syrup and butter together in a small saucepan, or in a small bowl in the microwave, until the butter is melted. Stack the pancakes on warmed plates and pour the buttery syrup over them.

If you don't want to make your own ice cream, use your favorite good quality store-bought vanilla ice cream, with maple syrup poured on top.

waffles with maple syrup ice cream

ice cream

2 cups heavy cream

1 cup milk

seeds from 1 vanilla bean

5 egg yolks

½ cup maple syrup

waffles

1 cup all-purpose flour

1 teaspoon baking powder

½ teaspoon baking soda

1 tablespoon sugar

½ cup buttermilk

1 egg, lightly beaten

6 tablespoons butter, melted

maple syrup, to serve

ice cream maker (optional)

waffle iron, lightly greased

serves 6

To make the ice cream, put the cream, milk, and vanilla seeds in a saucepan and heat until the mixture reaches boiling point. Remove the pan from the heat and set aside.

Meanwhile, beat the egg yolks and maple syrup together, then stir in the heated cream mixture and return to the pan. Heat gently, stirring, until the mixture thickens enough to coat the back of a wooden spoon. Do not boil or the mixture will curdle. Remove from the heat and let cool. Freeze in an ice cream maker, following the manufacturer's instructions. If you don't have an ice cream maker, pour the mixture into flat freezer trays and put them in the freezer. Let the mixture partially freeze, remove from the freezer, scoop into a bowl and beat to break up the ice crystals. Scoop back into the trays and return the trays to the freezer. Repeat several times—the more you do it, the smoother the end result.

To make the waffles, sift the flour, baking powder, and baking soda into a bowl. Stir in the sugar. Put the buttermilk, egg, and melted butter in a second bowl and beat well. Pour into the dry ingredients and beat until a smooth batter forms.

Spoon a layer of the batter onto a heated waffle iron and spread flat. Cook for about 1 minute until crisp and golden. If you don't have a waffle iron, then make into pancakes instead by simply dropping a ladle of batter onto a lightly greased, heated skillet and sauté until golden on both sides. Serve hot with a scoop of ice cream and a little extra maple syrup.

pecan and chocolate **muffins**

1½ cups self-rising flour

1 teaspoon baking powder

2½ oz. pecans, finely ground,
about ¾ cup

⅔ cup brown sugar

1 egg

¼ cup maple syrup

1 cup milk

4 tablespoons butter, melted

3¼ oz. dark chocolate, coarsely
chopped into very small pieces
about ½ cup

chopped pecans, to decorate

*one 12-cup muffin pan,
lined with paper muffin cups*

makes 12

Use good quality dark chocolate, chopped up, rather than chocolate chips, since it has a much better flavor and texture.

Sift the flour and baking powder into a bowl and stir in the pecans and sugar. Put the egg, maple syrup, milk, and melted butter in a second bowl and beat well. Pour into the dry ingredients and beat, then fold in the chocolate pieces.

Spoon the mixture into the paper cups, sprinkling the surface with extra chopped pecans.

Bake in a preheated oven at 400°F for 18–20 minutes, until risen and golden. Cool on a wire rack. Serve warm.

This recipe serves only two because it's not easy to cook more than this quantity at once. Make separate batches if there are more than two of you. If you can find wild mushrooms such as chanterelle or girolle, then you are in for a real treat.

scrambled eggs with mushrooms

8 oz. portobello mushrooms, or mixed wild mushrooms

6 free-range eggs

4 tablespoons unsalted butter

2 teaspoons chopped fresh thyme leaves

sea salt and freshly ground black pepper

to serve

fresh thyme leaves

toast

sautéed mushrooms (optional)

serves 2

Wipe the mushrooms with a damp cloth and cut into thick slices. Put the eggs in a bowl, add salt and pepper, to taste, and beat until blended.

Melt 3 tablespoons of the butter in a large skillet. As soon as it stops foaming, add the mushrooms, thyme, salt, and pepper. Sauté over medium heat until lightly browned and the juices are starting to run.

Push the mushrooms to one side of the pan, add the remaining butter, then pour in the beaten eggs, stirring with a fork until almost set.

Gradually stir in the mushrooms from the sides of the pan, cook a moment longer, then spoon onto serving plates. Sprinkle with thyme leaves and serve with toast and a few extra sautéed mushrooms, if using.

eggs benedict

If you sauté the prosciutto, it becomes really crisp, adding a lovely texture to the creamy sauce and egg yolks. Try replacing smoked salmon for the prosciutto or, for your vegetarian guests, replace it with some wilted spinach.

4 large slices of prosciutto
4 free range eggs
1–2 tablespoons vinegar, for poaching
4 English muffins

hollandaise sauce

1 cup (2 sticks) unsalted butter
3 egg yolks
2 tablespoons water
1 teaspoon freshly squeezed lemon juice
sea salt and cracked black pepper

serves 4

To make the hollandaise sauce, put the butter in a small saucepan and melt it gently over very low heat, without letting it brown. Put the egg yolks, water, and lemon juice in a blender and blend until frothy. With the blender running, gradually pour in the melted butter in a steady stream until the sauce is thickened and glossy. Transfer the sauce to a bowl set over a saucepan of hot water (or, if you have one, into the top pan of a double boiler). Cover and keep the sauce warm.

Broil or sauté the slices of prosciutto until really crisp, and keep them warm in a low oven. To poach the eggs, bring a saucepan of lightly salted water to a boil. Add 1 tablespoon vinegar, preferably distilled, and reduce to a gentle simmer. Swirl the water well with a fork and crack 2 eggs into the water. Cook for 3 minutes, remove with a slotted spoon, and repeat with the remaining 2 eggs.

Meanwhile, toast the muffins whole (not sliced) and top each one with a slice of crisp prosciutto. Put a poached egg on top of the prosciutto. Spoon the hollandaise sauce on top, sprinkle with salt and pepper, and serve at once.

french toast
with smoky bacon and spiked tomatoes

Day-old bread is best for this recipe since it will soak up more of the eggy mixture and cook better than fresh bread. The eggs make the bread puff up inside like a delicious soufflé.

Preheat the broiler. Put the eggs in a bowl and beat until mixed. Add plenty of salt and pepper. Pour the egg mixture into a large, shallow dish, then dip the slices of bread in the egg mixture, coating them all over, then set the dish aside for a few minutes to let the egg soak into the bread.

Meanwhile, broil the bacon for 1–2 minutes on each side until crisp. Transfer to a low oven to keep it warm.

Heat 1 tablespoon of the oil in a skillet until hot. Add the tomatoes and sprinkle with the sugar. Sauté for 1–2 minutes on each side until caramelized. Sprinkle with the chile oil and remove from the heat. Transfer to a plate and put in a very low oven to keep warm.

Wipe the skillet clean with paper towels, add the butter and remaining oil, and heat until hot. Add the egg-soaked bread, in batches if necessary, and sauté for 2 minutes on each side until crisp and golden.

Put 2 triangles of toast on each plate with 3 pieces of bacon on top. Spoon the tomatoes over the bacon, sprinkle with the basil, and serve immediately.

4 eggs

4 slices thick white bread, cut in half diagonally

12 slices of bacon

2 tablespoons olive oil

4 large plum tomatoes, cut in half lengthwise

2 teaspoons sugar

2 teaspoons chile oil

2 tablespoons butter

2 tablespoons basil leaves, torn

sea salt and freshly ground black pepper

serves 4

warm potato tortilla
with smoked salmon

1 lb. small new potatoes

2 tablespoons butter

1 small onion, sliced

4 eggs

8 oz. smoked salmon (lox)

sea salt and freshly ground black pepper

to serve

smoked salmon (lox)

salmon caviar

crème fraîche or sour cream

4 blini pans (optional)

serves 4

Tortillas make a great base for serving smoked salmon and eggs at a special brunch. You can make individual tortillas in little blini pans (sold in good cookware stores), but the dish is equally delicious when cooked in a large skillet and cut into wedges.

Cook the potatoes in a saucepan of lightly salted, boiling water for 10–12 minutes until cooked but not falling apart. Drain and refresh under cold water. Pat dry and cut into small cubes.

Put half the butter in a skillet, melt over low heat, add the onion, and cook gently for 5 minutes. Add the cubed potatoes and cook for 5 minutes more.

Put the eggs, salt, and pepper into a bowl, beat well, then stir in the potato and onion mixture. Put the remaining butter into 4 blini pans or 1 skillet, melt gently, then add the egg mixture.

Cook over gentle heat for 6–8 minutes, then flip the tortilla, or transfer to a preheated broiler, to set and lightly brown the surface. If making 1 large tortilla, cook it for about 10 minutes before broiling.

Let cool a little, then serve topped with smoked salmon, a little salmon caviar, and crème fraîche or sour cream.

appetizers

baked chèvre

Simple and delicious, this can be served as an appetizer or whipped up as a quick lunchtime snack for unexpected guests.

4 thick slices of goat cheese with rind (Bûcheron), 2 oz. per serving

extra virgin olive oil, for sprinkling

1 tablespoon chopped fresh thyme leaves

freshly ground black pepper

to serve

4 slices of sourdough bread

1–2 garlic cloves, cut in half

green salad

a baking tray, lined with foil

serves 4

Put the slices of goat cheese onto the prepared baking tray, sprinkle with a little oil, dot with thyme leaves, and season with pepper. Bake in a preheated oven at 400°F for 10–12 minutes until just starting to ooze and run.

Meanwhile, toast the sourdough and rub it with the cut garlic. When the cheese is ready, spread it onto the toasted, garlicky sourdough and serve with a green salad.

lemon potato latkes
with gingered avocado crème

2 large potatoes, about 1½ lb.

1 small onion, finely chopped

grated zest of 1 unwaxed lemon

2 teaspoons freshly squeezed
lemon juice

¼ cup all-purpose flour

¼ teaspoon baking powder

1 teaspoon kosher salt or sea salt

olive oil, for frying

gingered avocado crème

1 large ripe avocado, cut in half
and pitted

freshly squeezed juice of 1 lime

1–2 teaspoons finely grated
fresh ginger

½ teaspoon crushed garlic

1 red serrano chile, seeded and finely
chopped, or 1 tablespoon chile sauce

1 tablespoon soy sauce

2 tablespoons plain yogurt

makes 20–24, serves 4

Though rather indulgent, sautéed potato pancakes are worth every mouthful. Keep them small and they'll cook in minutes. Eat them right away or reheat in a hot oven for five minutes.

To make the latkes, peel the potatoes, then grate on the coarse side of a box grater or in a food processor. Transfer to a strainer and let drain. Press excess moisture out of the potatoes (or they will "spit" when cooked) and put them in a bowl. Add the onion, lemon zest and juice, flour, baking powder, and salt to the bowl and mix well. Return the mixture to the strainer—liquid will continue to drain out of the mixture while you prepare to cook the latkes.

Heat about ¼-inch depth of olive oil in a skillet. Add rounded tablespoons of the mixture and flatten slightly—don't overcrowd the pan. Sauté for 2–3 minutes on each side until golden and crisp. Remove with a slotted spoon and drain on crumpled paper towels. Keep the latkes warm in the oven while you cook the remaining batches.

To make the avocado crème, scoop the avocado flesh into a bowl and mash with a fork. Add the remaining ingredients and beat until smooth. Serve with the latkes.

This makes an elegant appetizer to serve to friends. The cream has a punchy pepper kick to it with cool lemon undertones. Tossing the salmon in the dill gives it a lovely fresh appearance.

smoked salmon
and lemon pepper cream crostini

½ lb. thinly sliced smoked salmon (lox)

2 tablespoons chopped fresh dill

sea salt

crostini

1 thin French baguette, thinly sliced diagonally

extra virgin olive oil, for brushing

lemon pepper cream

2 teaspoons black peppercorns

⅓ cup mascarpone cheese

⅓ cup milk

finely grated zest and juice of 1 unwaxed lemon

a baking tray

serves 6

To make the crostini, brush both sides of each slice of bread with olive oil, and spread out on a baking tray. Bake in a preheated oven at 375°F for about 10 minutes until crisp and golden. Let cool, then keep in an airtight container until ready to use. It is best to reheat them in the oven before adding the topping.

To make the lemon pepper cream, pound or grind the peppercorns as finely as possible. Beat the mascarpone with the ground pepper, add the milk and lemon zest, and beat again. Season with salt and lemon juice to taste. Chill until needed.

Toss the smoked salmon with the chopped dill. Spread the crostini with the lemon pepper cream and put a mound of smoked salmon on top. Squeeze a little more lemon juice over it and serve immediately.

grilled polenta with grilled bell peppers

This recipe uses quick-cook polenta to save time. You can prepare the polenta and the basil oil the day before, leaving you very little to do when your guests arrive.

1 package quick-cook polenta, about 4 oz.

2 tablespoons butter

kosher salt or sea salt and freshly ground black pepper

sprigs of basil and oregano, to serve

basil oil

1 large bunch of basil

½ cup extra virgin olive oil

char-grilled bell peppers

6 red or yellow bell peppers, preferably long peppers, cut in half and seeded

olive oil, for coating

a removable-bottomed cake pan, oiled

serves 8

Prepare the polenta according to the package instructions, stir in the butter, then pour into the oiled cake pan. Let cool and set. Chill until ready to grill.

To make the basil oil, put the basil in a food processor and pulse until finely chopped. With the blender running, add the oil gradually through the feed tube, then add a pinch of salt. Chill for at least 30 minutes, or preferably overnight to intensify the flavor and color. Strain through a fine strainer into a small pitcher.

To cook the bell peppers, put the halves or pieces in a plastic bag, add some olive oil, along with some salt and pepper, and shake to coat with oil. Heat a stove-top grill pan over medium heat until hot. Remove the peppers from the bag and add them, skin side down, to the grill pan. Put a heavy weight, such as a large saucepan, on top, and cook until dark and charred with marks. Turn the pieces over, put the saucepan back on top and cook until tender. Use as they are, or, to remove the skins, transfer the peppers to a small saucepan, cover it, and let it sit— the skins will gently steam off and you won't lose any delicious juices.

Turn the polenta out of the cake pan and cut into 8 wedges. Reheat the grill pan, then brush the polenta wedges with olive oil, add to the pan, and cook until barred with brown on one side. Turn the pieces over and cook the other side until hot, golden, and browned. Transfer to warm plates, top with the peppers, drizzle with basil oil and any pepper juices, add sprigs of basil and oregano, and serve.

Shrimp are very popular as an appetizer. Some of them are striped gray or blue; others have silvery shells or look pink or translucent. This recipe suits almost any variety of shrimp—adjust the cooking time to suit the size. Tails alone cook more quickly than whole shrimp.

shrimp with parsley and lemon

1¼ lb. large, unpeeled shrimp, washed

2 tablespoons sea salt

1 tablespoon red wine vinegar

4 large sprigs of flat-leaf parsley, leaves pinched off and chopped (optional), stalks finely chopped

freshly squeezed juice of 2 lemons

2 tablespoons extra virgin olive oil

2 lemons, cut in half, to serve (optional)

serves 4

To devein the shrimp, cut a slit down the back into the flesh and discard any black threads. Put 1 cup water into a saucepan, add the salt, and bring to a boil. Add the shrimp, and stir in the vinegar and half the parsley stalks. Return to a boil, reduce the heat, and cook gently for 2–4 minutes, stirring the shrimp now and then, until their flesh turns dense, white, and firm. The shells may change color, often to pink or scarlet.

Remove the cooked shrimp to a serving dish. Take 2 tablespoons of the cooking liquid and put it in a small pitcher. Add the lemon juice, oil, the remaining parlsey stalks, and parsley leaves, if using, and mix well. Pour this over the shrimp. Let cool, then put in the refrigerator to marinate for 10–20 minutes.

Serve with the lemon halves, paper napkins, finger bowls, and containers for the discarded shrimp shells.

trout fishcakes

Moist, with a lovely, earthy flavor, trout is perfect for making fishcakes. The cakes need to be chilled so they will keep their shape when fried.

Put the potatoes in a saucepan, cover with water, and bring to a boil. Add the salt and simmer gently for 15 minutes, until the potatoes are tender.

Meanwhile, put the fish in a large, shallow saucepan and pour the milk over it. Cover, bring to a boil, reduce the heat, and simmer gently for 5–6 minutes, until the fish is opaque all the way through and just cooked. Using a slotted spoon, remove to a plate and let cool. Remove and discard the skin, then coarsely flake.

Drain the potatoes and return them to the pan. Add the butter and mash until smooth. Put in a large bowl, add the parsley and chives, and mix. Add plenty of salt and pepper. Using a large metal spoon, gently fold in the flaked fish.

Using floured hands, shape the mixture into 4 round cakes, about 1 inch thick. Dip them first into the beaten egg, and then into the bread crumbs to coat all over. Refrigerate for 30 minutes.

Pour ¾ inch oil into a large skillet and heat until hot. Add the fishcakes and sauté over medium heat for 3–4 minutes on each side, until golden brown and heated through.

To blanch the beans, bring a saucepan of water to a boil, add the beans, and boil for 2–3 minutes, until they turn bright green. Drain, run under cold water, and drain again. Toss the beans and spinach together in a bowl, divide between 4 plates, and put a fishcake on top. Serve with extra chives and tartar sauce.

1 lb. potatoes, cut into small chunks, about 3–3½ cups

½ teaspoon salt

1 lb. rainbow trout fillets

1 cup milk

2 tablespoons butter

a small bunch of flat-leaf parsley, chopped

a small bunch of chives, chopped

flour, for flouring our hands

1 egg, beaten

2½ cups fresh white bread crumbs

canola or safflower oil, for cooking

4 oz. thin green beans, blanched and refreshed

1 cup baby spinach leaves

sea salt and freshly ground black pepper

to serve (optional)

extra chives

tartar sauce

serves 4

bresaola and arugula
with olive oil and parmesan

This is quick and simple appetizer provides a truly delicious combination of flavors. Bresaola is Italian cured beef—flavorful, deep crimson, lean, and succulent. Preferably it should be cut in very thin slices from a whole piece, but it is also available presliced, in packages. Serve it cool.

12–16 thin slices of bresaola

2 oz. Parmesan cheese
(about 1 cup shavings)

a large handful of arugula, torn

4–6 teaspoons high-quality
extra virgin olive oil

serves 4

Arrange the slices of bresaola on 4 serving plates.

Using a swivel-bladed vegetable peeler or sharp knife, shave off thin curls of Parmesan and sprinkle them on top of the bresaola.

Add the arugula, then drizzle with extra virgin olive oil, and serve immediately.

These wraps are a hands-on appetizer and always go down well. The paper wrappers keep them moist and stop them sticking together if you want to prepare them in advance. Chinese pancakes are sold by Chinese grocers—in the frozen food section or refrigerated case.

peking-style duck pancake wraps

4 duck breasts, 6 oz. each

1 tablespoon salt

¼ cup dark soy sauce

1 tablespoon honey

2 teaspoons 5-spice powder

1 tablespoon peanut oil

to serve

1 cucumber, about 12 inches long

24 Chinese pancakes

½ cup hoisin sauce

6 scallions, cut in half lengthwise and crosswise

sweet chile sauce (optional)

24 squares of parchment paper or wax paper, 5 x 5 inches

makes 24

Score the duck fat diagonally at ⅛ inch intervals and rub in the salt. Mix the soy sauce, honey, and 5-spice powder in a shallow dish. Put the duck breasts, skin side up, in the marinade, moving them around so the flesh is coated. Marinate in the refrigerator for at least 2 hours.

Remove the duck from the marinade and pat dry with paper towels.

Heat the oil in a skillet, add the duck breasts, skin side down, and cook for 8 minutes. Pour off the fat from the skillet, then turn the breasts and cook the other side for 4 minutes. Let cool, then slice each duck breast diagonally into 6 strips.

Quarter the cucumber lengthwise, and scoop out and discard the seeds. Slice each quarter into 6 pieces lengthwise, and then in half crosswise. You should have 48 pieces.

Steam the pancakes for 5 minutes over boiling water. To assemble, work on 3–4 pancakes at a time and keep the others covered so they don't dry out. Spread 1 teaspoon hoisin sauce on each pancake, add a piece of duck, a few strips of cucumber, and a piece of scallion. Fold up the bottom, then fold in the sides. Wrap a piece of paper around each pancake in the same way. Cover with a cloth until ready to serve.

soup

celery root, saffron, and orange soup with parsley gremolata

2 tablespoons butter or olive oil

1 large onion, chopped

1 celery root, about 1½ lb., peeled and cut into cubes, about 6 cups (make up the weight with potatoes, if necessary)

4 cups vegetable stock

½ teaspoon saffron strands, lightly ground with a mortar and pestle

1 tablespoon honey

grated zest and freshly squeezed juice of 1 large unwaxed orange

sea salt and freshly ground black pepper

sour cream or plain yogurt, to serve

parsley gremolata

1 garlic clove

1 teaspoon sea salt

a handful of fresh flat-leaf parsley

2 tablespoons olive oil

serves 4

An elegant, rich soup, which can also be made dairy-free for vegans—use olive oil instead of butter, and leave out the sour cream or yogurt. Although the parsley gremolata is optional, it lifts both the color and flavor.

Heat the butter or oil in a saucepan, add the onion, and cook until softened. Add the celery root and potato, if using, cover, and cook for 10 minutes, stirring occasionally. Add the stock, saffron, honey, orange zest and juice, salt, and pepper. Bring to a boil and simmer for 20 minutes until the vegetables are tender. Purée the soup either in the pan, using a hand-held stick immersion blender, or in a blender or food processor, in batches if necessary. Purée until smooth.

To make the gremolata, put all the ingredients in a food processor or spice grinder, and blend until smooth. Alternatively, grind using a mortar and pestle.

To serve, ladle the soup into warmed bowls, and spoon the gremolata on top, if using, along with some sour cream or yogurt.

This is a quintessentially American soup, popular in both North and South America. The key to this soup is the light spicing and the roasting of the butternut squash to bring out the best of its sweet flavor.

butternut squash soup
with allspice and pine nuts

1 medium butternut squash, cut in half lengthwise, and seeded

2 tablespoons unsalted butter

1 large leek, trimmed and chopped

1 bay leaf

a few black peppercorns, crushed

4–5 allspice berries, crushed

2¾ cups vegetable stock

½ cup pine nuts, toasted in a dry skillet

crusty bread, to serve

a nonstick baking tray

serves 4

Put the butternut squash halves, flesh side down, onto the baking tray. Roast in a preheated oven at 375°F for 45 minutes or until tender. Remove from the oven and, using a spoon, scoop the flesh out of the skins and into a bowl. Discard the skins.

Put the butter in a large saucepan and melt over medium to low heat. Add the chopped leek, bay leaf, peppercorns, and allspice, and sauté until the leek begins to soften. Add the butternut squash, stock, and 1 quart water. Bring to a boil, reduce the heat, and simmer for about 10 minutes, or until the leeks are very soft.

Remove and discard the bay leaf, and transfer the soup to a blender or food processor. Add the pine nuts and blend until smooth, working in batches if necessary. Return the soup to the saucepan and reheat. Serve hot with crusty bread.

This soup is simplicity itself. There may seem to be a lot of mushrooms in it, but they shrink considerably when cooked, and release their flavorful juices into the aromatic broth.

portobello soup
with madeira and thyme

2 tablespoons butter

1 onion, chopped

2 garlic cloves, chopped

10 oz. shiitake mushrooms, torn or chopped into big chunks (about 2½–3 cups)

10 oz. portobello or other large mushrooms, torn or chopped into big chunks (about 2½–3 cups)

2 cups vegetable stock

⅔ cup Madeira wine or dry sherry

a bunch of fresh thyme, tied with kitchen twine

kosher salt or sea salt and freshly ground black pepper

to serve

heavy cream

chopped parsley

serves 4

Melt the butter in a large saucepan, add the onion, and cook over low heat until softened and translucent. Add the garlic, mushrooms, salt, and pepper. Increase the heat, cover, and cook, stirring occasionally, until the mushrooms have softened and their juices have been released, about 5 minutes.

Pour in the stock, and Madeira or sherry, and drop in the bundle of thyme. Bring to a boil, then cover and simmer for 15 minutes. Remove the thyme. Coarsely purée the soup, either in the pan, using a hand-held stick immersion blender, or in a blender or food processor, in batches if necessary. Return the soup to the pan and reheat. Ladle into warmed bowls, top with a swirl of cream, chopped parsley, and lots of black pepper, and serve.

Ice-cold and enhanced with avocado, lime, cumin, and chili powder, this soup is refreshingly hard to beat on a hot summer's day. For a special occasion, freeze cilantro leaves in ice cubes, and use them to give your soup a decorative finish.

mexican gazpacho

2 garlic cloves

1 teaspoon sea salt

1 large cucumber, peeled and coarsely chopped

1 yellow bell pepper, seeded and coarsely chopped

2 celery stalks, coarsely chopped

4 ripe tomatoes, coarsely chopped

1 red onion, coarsely chopped

4 cups fresh tomato juice

2 teaspoons cumin seeds, pan-toasted

1 teaspoon mild chili powder

1 ripe avocado, cut in half and pitted

freshly squeezed juice of 2 limes

freshly ground black pepper

cilantro leaves set in ice cubes, or chopped cilantro, to serve

serves 6

Using a mortar and pestle, pound the garlic with the salt until well mashed. Put the cucumber, bell pepper, celery, tomatoes, and onion in a bowl, add the mashed garlic, and mix well.

Transfer half of the mixture to a food processor and pulse until chopped but still slightly chunky, and then scoop it into a bowl. Spoon the remaining mixture into a food processor and blend until smooth. Add this to the chunky mixture in the bowl. Mix in the tomato juice, cumin, chili powder, and pepper, to taste.

Chill in the refrigerator for several hours until very cold, or overnight. If short of time, put the soup in the freezer for 30 minutes to chill.

Cut the avocado into small cubes, toss in the lime juice until well coated, then stir into the chilled gazpacho.

To serve, ladle the soup into chilled bowls, then add a few cilantro-leaf ice cubes or sprinkle with chopped cilantro.

andalusian chickpea soup
with chorizo, paprika, and saffron

2 tablespoons extra virgin olive oil

1 medium onion, chopped

3 thin celery stalks, chopped, with leaves reserved

1 large carrot, chopped

2 garlic cloves, chopped

8 oz. chorizo sausage, skinned, cut in half lengthwise, then cut into ½-inch slices (or use a mixture of chorizo and another Southern European sausage, such as morcilla or Italian sausages)

15 oz. canned chickpeas, rinsed and drained

7 cups chicken stock

¼ teaspoon hot pimentón (Spanish oak-smoked paprika)

4 oz. spinach, tough stalks removed and leaves coarsely chopped into large pieces, about 1 cup

¼ teaspoon saffron threads, bruised with a mortar and pestle

Manchego or Parmesan cheese, shaved, to serve (optional)

serves 4 as an entrée

This hearty soup is a meal in itself. The special flavor comes from two typically Spanish spices, pimentón (Spanish oak-smoked paprika, made from a variety of bell pepper) and its home-grown luxury spice, saffron.

Heat the oil in a large saucepan and add the onion, celery, and carrot. Gently sauté the vegetables until they begin to soften. Add the garlic, chorizo, chickpeas, stock, and paprika. Bring to a boil, reduce the heat, and simmer for about 10 minutes. Add the spinach and celery leaves and simmer for 15 minutes more.

Add the saffron and clean out the mortar using a little of the stock (so as not to waste any of the expensive saffron). Add to the saucepan and simmer for another 5 minutes.

Serve hot in large warm bowls as an entrée. Add shavings of cheese, if using. This soup is very filling, but serve some good crusty bread, and perhaps some extra cheese, alongside if your guests are hungry.

5 cups chicken stock

12 oz. boneless, skinless chicken breasts, thinly sliced

2 garlic cloves, chopped

2 stalks of lemongrass, cut in half lengthwise

3 tablespoons Thai fish sauce or light soy sauce

2 inches fresh ginger root, peeled and grated

8 small scallions, quartered

½ cup coconut cream

4 fresh kaffir lime leaves, crushed (optional)

2 green bird's eye chiles, crushed

a large handful of fresh cilantro leaves, torn

8 oz. raw tiger shrimp, peeled or unpeeled*

freshly squeezed juice of 2 limes

serves 4

*Do not use cooked shrimp: the texture will be disappointing. Use cubes of other fresh fish instead.

This is one of the world's best-loved soups. Ingredients like lemongrass and kaffir lime leaves are sold fresh in supermarkets as part of the packs of fresh Thai herbs and flavorings. If unavailable, avoid dried versions from the spice rack—they're just not intense and aromatic enough—use fresh lemon and lime zest instead.

spicy thai chicken soup

Put the stock into a large saucepan and bring to a boil. Add the chicken, garlic, lemongrass, fish sauce or light soy sauce, ginger, scallions, and coconut cream.

Return to a boil, partially cover, reduce the heat to a high simmer, and cook for 5 minutes. Add the kaffir lime leaves, if using, the chiles, half the cilantro leaves, and the shrimp.

Simmer gently for 5 minutes or until the chicken is cooked through and the shrimp flesh is densely white—do not overcook or the shrimp will be tough. Add the lime juice and serve in warmed soup bowls, topped with the remaining cilantro leaves.

salads

A green salad is the easiest of dishes to assemble, but, to be successful, the ingredients must be very good quality. Choose a selection of greens (soft and crisp, sweet and bitter), then dress them with the best extra virgin olive oil, the lightest touch of vinegar or lemon juice, and just the right amount of seasoning.

fresh green salad

2 handfuls of peppery leaves, such as arugula or watercress

2 handfuls of bitter leaves, such as chicory

2 handfuls of crisp lettuce, such as romaine or Bibb lettuce, torn

1 small head of Belgian endive, separated into leaves

leaves from a small bunch of flat-leaf parsley, dill, or mint (optional)

1 small onion, thinly sliced into rings

dressing

2 garlic cloves, crushed

½ teaspoon salt

1–1½ tablespoons freshly squeezed lemon juice

½–⅓ cup extra virgin olive oil

serves 4

To make the dressing, put the garlic, salt, and half the lemon juice in a small bowl and mix with a hand-held stick blender. Slowly pour in the oil and blend until emulsified. Taste, then add enough lemon juice to give bite.

Alternatively, use a mortar and pestle to pound the garlic and salt to a sticky paste. Slowly pour in the oil, continuing to pound and stir until a rich emulsion forms. Add lemon juice to taste.

Put the washed leaves, herbs, if using, and onion rings in a large bowl, cover with a plastic bag, seal, and chill until ready to serve, so the leaves stay crisp and fresh.

Just before serving, trickle the dressing over the leaves and toss thoroughly with your hands or wooden spoons.

The secret of this salad is to have the walnuts sizzling hot. Get the salad ready and add the walnuts as soon as they come out of the oven. Walnut oil is great in dressings, but just use extra olive oil if you can't find it. Keep nuts and nut oils (except peanut oil) in the refrigerator, because they can go rancid quickly.

belgian endive, chicory, and radicchio salad with walnut dressing

1 cup walnuts

1 teaspoon walnut oil

1 teaspoon sea salt

1 head of radicchio, leaves separated, washed, and dried

2 heads of Belgian endive, leaves separated, washed, and dried

1 small chicory, leaves separated, washed, and dried

walnut dressing

1 tablespoon walnut oil

1 tablespoon extra virgin olive oil

a good squeeze of fresh lemon juice

freshly ground black pepper

a baking tray

serves 4

Put the walnuts, walnut oil, and salt in a small bowl and stir. Scoop into a baking tray, in a single layer, and cook in a preheated oven at 400°F for 8–10 minutes, until toasted all over.

Meanwhile, put the salad greens in a large salad bowl. To make the dressing, put the oils and lemon juice in a separate bowl and beat well. Add freshly ground black pepper to taste.

To serve, sprinkle the hot walnuts over the salad greens, pour the dressing on top, and toss well. Serve immediately as a salad, or with crusty bread and shavings of Parmesan as a lunch or salad appetizer.

Insalata Caprese is a favorite Italian salad, sporting the colors of the national flag and just the simplest of dressings. There is nothing better than a little ground sea salt and pepper, and the traditional healthy sprinkling of the best extra virgin olive oil.

mozzarella, tomato, and basil salad

1 lb. fresh mozzarella cheese, preferably buffalo, sliced or torn

8 plum tomatoes on the vine, such as Roma or San Marzano, thickly sliced

a large handful of basil leaves

extra virgin olive oil, for sprinkling

balsamic vinegar, for sprinkling (optional)

sea salt and freshly ground black pepper

Italian bread, such as ciabatta, to serve

serves 4

Put about 3 slices or chunks of mozzarella on each plate. Add 3 slices of tomato, sprinkle with salt and pepper, then top with basil (basil should be torn, not cut, for the best flavor and appearance).

Alternatively, arrange the tomato and mozzarella slices in lines on a large serving platter, then add salt, pepper, and basil leaves as before.

Sprinkle olive oil generously over the salad, then add a few drops of balsamic vinegar, if using, and serve with plenty of Italian bread.

This classic salad never seems to lose its appeal and is constantly being updated. The original recipe calls for barely-cooked eggs, but boiled eggs, cooked until the yolks are just set, make a fantastic dressing. For this vegetarian alternative, anchovies have been replaced with vegetarian Worcestershire sauce.

vegetarian caesar salad

1 romaine lettuce, outer leaves removed, or 2 small lettuce hearts

freshly grated Parmesan cheese, to serve

croutons

2 thick slices white bread, cubed

1 tablespoon olive oil

dressing

2 eggs

¼ cup freshly grated Parmesan cheese

3 tablespoons white wine vinegar

2 teaspoons vegetarian Worcestershire sauce

1 tablespoon chopped chives (optional)

¼ cup olive oil

sea salt and freshly ground black pepper

a baking tray

serves 4–6

To make the croutons, put the cubes of bread in a bowl, drizzle with the olive oil, and toss until evenly coated. Tip onto a baking tray and bake in a preheated oven at 375°F until golden and crisp on all sides, about 10 minutes. Check the bread occasionally while cooking, so it doesn't burn. Let cool.

To make the dressing, put the eggs in a saucepan of cold water and bring to a boil. Cook for 5–6 minutes, then drain immediately and cool under cold running water. Peel the eggs when cold, then put them in a small bowl and mash with a fork. Add the remaining dressing ingredients, except the oil, and whisk thoroughly. Gradually add the oil—a little at a time—whisking until emulsified.

Tear the lettuce into pieces and put them in a large bowl, pour the dressing on top, and toss until well coated. Top with the croutons, sprinkle with Parmesan, and serve.

warm chickpea salad
with spiced mushrooms

This entrée salad was inspired by Middle Eastern cuisine, where beans, yogurt, and mint are widely used. Make this dish more substantial by serving it on a bed of couscous or bulgur wheat. The convenience of canned chickpeas may appeal if you don't have time to soak and cook the dried variety. You shouldn't notice much difference in taste, if any.

3 tablespoons olive oil

12 oz. button mushrooms (about 4 cups)

2 garlic cloves, chopped

1 red serrano chile, seeded and chopped

15 oz. canned chickpeas, rinsed and drained

2 teaspoons ground cumin

freshly squeezed juice of 1 lemon

¾ cup plain yogurt

a large handful of mint leaves, chopped

8 oz. baby spinach leaves, about 5 cups

sea salt and freshly ground black pepper

serves 4

Heat 2 tablespoons of the oil a skillet. Add the mushrooms, season with salt, and cook until softened. Reduce the heat, then add the garlic, chile, and chickpeas. Sauté for 2 minutes, then add the cumin and half the lemon juice. Cook until the juices in the skillet evaporate, then remove from the heat and set aside.

Put the yogurt in a bowl, then add the chopped mint and the remaining lemon juice and oil. Add salt and pepper, to taste and mix until blended. Divide the spinach between 4 plates, or put all of it on a serving platter, add the chickpea and mushroom mixture, then pour the yogurt dressing over the top and serve.

This salad is packed with lovely flavors. When you serve lobster, the effect is instantly luxurious and "special occasion." Who would ever guess the dish was so simple to prepare? Make the mayonnaise if you have the time, as the result will be superior to any store-bought alternative.

lobster and fennel salad

1 large bulb of fennel

freshly squeezed juice of ½ lemon

¼ cup extra virgin olive oil

4 small cooked lobsters, about 1 lb. each, or 2 large ones

sea salt and freshly ground black pepper

mayonnaise

2 egg yolks

2 teaspoons white wine vinegar or freshly squeezed lemon juice

¼ teaspoon salt

2 teaspoons Dijon mustard

1¼ cups extra virgin olive oil

serves 4

To make the mayonnaise, put the egg yolks, vinegar or lemon juice, salt, and mustard in a blender or food processor, and blend briefly until frothy. With the blender running, drizzle the oil in through the funnel until the sauce is thick and glossy. It may be necessary to thin the mayonnaise slightly by blending in 1–2 tablespoons boiling water. Season to taste with pepper. Scoop into a bowl or clean jar, cover tightly, and store in the refrigerator for up to 5 days.

Trim off and discard the tough outer layer of fennel, then chop and reserve the fronds. Cut the bulb in half, then crosswise into very thin slices. Put in a bowl, add the lemon juice, oil, fennel fronds, salt, and pepper, toss well, then marinate for 15 minutes.

Cut the lobsters in half and lift the tail flesh out of the shell. Crack the claws with a small hammer or crab crackers, and carefully remove all the meat.

Put a layer of shaved fennel salad on each plate, top with the lobster, and serve with a spoonful of mayonnaise.

The availability of quality fresh tuna has made it one of today's most popular fish. It is a joy to cook and eat.

seared tuna salad
with lime and soy dressing

10 oz. fresh tuna steak

3 Belgian endive, leaves separated

2 bunches of watercress or spinach

dressing

grated zest and freshly squeezed juice of 2 unwaxed limes, plus extra wedges, to serve

1 chile, finely chopped

⅓ cup light soy sauce

2 fresh kaffir lime leaves, thinly sliced

1 stalk of fresh lemongrass, very thinly sliced

3 tablespoons olive oil

sea salt and freshly ground black pepper

serves 8

Heat a stove-top grill pan until very hot, then add the tuna steak. Cook for 2–3 minutes on each side. Don't move it around before this time, or it will not have formed a good crust and will break up. Remove to a carving board and let rest.

To make the dressing, put the lime zest and juice in a bowl. Add the chile, soy sauce, kaffir lime leaves, lemongrass, oil, salt, and pepper. Arrange the endive leaves on serving plates.

Cut the tuna crosswise into thin slices and arrange on top of the salad. Add the watercress and wedges of lime, spoon the dressing over the top, and serve.

Prosciutto makes the best crispy bacon any kitchen can produce, so start cooking and impress with this simple but delicious salad.

roasted eggplant and prosciutto salad

8 oz. cherry tomatoes, about 1½ cups

2 small eggplants, sliced lengthwise

2 tablespoons olive oil

4 slices prosciutto

a bunch of arugula

sea salt and freshly ground black pepper

dressing

1 tablespoon balsamic vinegar

1 tablespoon Dijon mustard

3 tablespoons extra virgin olive oil

a roasting pan, oiled

serves 4

Slice off and discard the top of each tomato, then put them, cut side up, in the roasting pan. Add the eggplant. Sprinkle with the olive oil, salt, and pepper. Cook in a preheated oven at 350°F for 15 minutes, then reduce to 300°F for a further 15 minutes, until the tomatoes have burst their skins. Remove from the oven and set aside.

Cook the prosciutto under a preheated hot broiler for about 3 minutes on each side, until crisp.

To make the dressing, put the vinegar and mustard in a small bowl and mix until smooth. Gradually add the oil, mixing well, then add salt and pepper to taste. Arrange the arugula, roasted eggplant, and tomatoes on 4 plates, and spoon the dressing over them. Top with the crispy prosciutto, and serve warm or at room temperature.

This salad makes a wonderful appetizer or late-night snack. Be careful not to overcook the chicken livers, or they will become dry and tough, not juicy and soft. Chicken livers are available from butchers and large supermarkets, fresh or frozen.

chicken liver salad

4 slices toasted or fried bread
8 oz. mixed salad greens
8 oz. chicken livers, about 1 cup
4 tablespoons butter
2 tablespoons olive oil
½ cup red wine
sea salt and freshly ground black pepper

serves 4

Put the toast on 4 small salad plates and top with the mixed salad greens.

Trim the chicken livers, removing any tubes and any dark or slightly green patches. Cut the livers into equal pieces.

Melt the butter and olive oil in a large saucepan. When really hot, add the chicken livers and cook for 2 minutes on one side, then turn them over and cook for 2 minutes more.

Add salt and pepper, then carefully remove the livers from the saucepan, using a slotted spoon, and divide them between the plates, laying them on top of the greens.

Add the wine to the pan juices and bring to a boil, stirring. Boil hard for 1 minute, then pour the hot dressing over the livers and serve.

3 mild or spicy chorizo sausages, about 4 oz. in total, cut crosswise into coin-shaped slices, or a 6 oz. piece, cut into chunks

12–16 baby zucchinis, cut in half lengthwise, about 10 oz.

1 lb. boneless, skinless, cooked or smoked chicken, cut or pulled into long strips

8 oz. loosely packed mixed red and green lettuce leaves (about 4 cups)

a handful of arugula or watercress

16–20 black olives, about 3 oz.

sprigs of cilantro or flat-leaf parsley

garlic bread, toasted ciabatta, or warmed focaccia, to serve

vinaigrette

2 tablespoons balsamic vinegar

⅓ cup extra virgin olive oil

2 garlic cloves, crushed

sea salt and freshly ground black pepper

serves 4

Chorizo—Spanish salami—adds extra pizzazz to many dishes. I like to sauté it first to release all the smoky paprika juices. Nothing could be simpler, or have more impact. It's available from many supermarkets and most good gourmet stores.

warm chicken
and chorizo salad

Heat a nonstick skillet or stove-top grill pan, add the chorizo slices or chunks, and sauté gently on all sides until the juices run and the edges are slightly crisp. Set aside.

Put the vinaigrette ingredients in a small bowl or measuring cup and mix well. Use some of the mixture to brush the zucchini halves, then add them to the still-hot pan and cook for 5 minutes on each side or until hot and golden.

Put the chicken in a large salad bowl, then add the lettuce leaves, rocket or watercress, and olives. Sprinkle with the remaining vinaigrette, then add the zucchini, the chorizo and its juices, and the cilantro or parsley. Toss well, then serve immediately with your choice of bread.

A summery way of enjoying roast beef without too much heat from the kitchen. Parboiling the potatoes before roasting means that they won't dry out and shrivel as they roast.

seared peppered beef salad
with horseradish dressing

1 lb. baby new potatoes, unpeeled

2 tablespoons olive oil

8 oz. baby plum tomatoes

4 beef tenderloin steaks, 4 oz. each

1 tablespoon Worcestershire sauce

2 cups arugula

1 cup sugar snap peas, trimmed, blanched, refreshed, and cut in half lengthwise

sea salt and freshly ground black pepper

horseradish dressing

3 tablespoons crème fraîche or sour cream

1–2 tablespoons horseradish

a squeeze of fresh lemon juice

serves 4

Bring a large saucepan of water to the boil, add the potatoes and par-boil for 8–10 minutes, until nearly cooked through. Drain and transfer to a roasting pan. Drizzle with 1 tablespoon olive oil and toss to coat. Sprinkle with salt and black pepper, and roast in a preheated oven at 425°F for 25–30 minutes, until browned and starting to crisp.

Remove from the oven and, using a large metal spoon, push the potatoes to one end of the pan, in a pile. Put the baby plum tomatoes into the empty half of the pan and sprinkle with 1 tablespoon olive oil, salt, and pepper. Roast in the oven for 15 minutes, until just soft.

Meanwhile, put all the dressing ingredients in a bowl and mix. Add salt and pepper to taste. Sprinkle the steaks with plenty of pepper and drizzle with the Worcestershire sauce. Preheat a stove-top grill pan, add the beef, and sear for 1–2 minutes on each side or until cooked to your liking. Set aside to rest.

Put the arugula and the sugar snap peas in a bowl and toss. Divide between 4 plates. Spoon the potatoes and tomatoes around the arugula and peas.

Slice the steaks diagonally and arrange the slices over the salad. Top with a dollop of horseradish dressing and serve, with any remaining sauce served separately.

vegetables &
vegetarian entrées

baked eggplant and tomato stacks

1 eggplant, about 8 oz., sliced into 12 thick rounds

1 large beefsteak tomato, about 6 oz., sliced into 8 rounds

8 oz. Taleggio cheese, or any other good melting cheese, cut into 12 slices

crisp green salad or lightly steamed vegetables, to serve

extra virgin olive oil, for brushing and sprinkling

a ceramic baking dish, oiled

serves 4

This is a filling vegetarian dish, topped with bubbly, browned cheese. Taleggio—full of nuttiness when melted—is used here, but try any other good melting cheese, such as Fontina, Gruyère, or mozzarella. Beefsteak tomatoes are perfect for this dish as they are delightfully large and easy to slice and stack.

Lightly brush a skillet with the oil and heat until hot. Working in batches, add the eggplant slices and cook for a few minutes on each side until browned and slightly soft.

To make the stacks, arrange 4 slices of eggplant apart in the baking dish. Add 1 slice of tomato to each one, then 1 slice of cheese. Repeat until each stack has 3 slices of eggplant, 2 of tomato, and 3 of cheese, ending with a cheese slice on top. Sprinkle each stack with olive oil.

Bake in a preheated oven at 375°F for about 15 minutes until soft, bubbly, and golden. Serve hot with a crisp green salad or lightly steamed vegetables.

provençal tian

A tian is a shallow clay dish in the language of Provence and also anything cooked in it. Vegetables such as tomatoes and zucchini are prone to losing a lot of liquid, so it's a good idea to remove some liquid beforehand by roasting or salting (this is known as "degorging").

6 large ripe tomatoes, cut in half

4 garlic cloves, thinly sliced

6 small eggplants, thickly sliced lengthwise

3 zucchinis or yellow squash, thickly sliced lengthwise

⅓ cup olive oil, plus extra for brushing

2 large red onions, thickly sliced

2 tablespoons chopped fresh thyme leaves

sea salt and freshly ground black pepper

sprigs of basil, to serve (optional)

topping

grated zest of 1 unwaxed lemon

3 garlic cloves, crushed

about 1 cup dried bread crumbs

½ cup freshly grated Parmesan cheese

a baking tray

a tian or other shallow ceramic ovenproof dish

serves 4–6

Put the tomatoes on a baking tray, cut side up, and push slivers of garlic into each one. Roast in a preheated oven at 400°F for about 30 minutes in order to remove some of the moisture.

Meanwhile, put the eggplants and zucchinis or squash on a plate, sprinkle with salt, and set aside for 30 minutes to extract some of the moisture. Rinse and pat dry with paper towels.

Heat the oil in a large skillet, add the onions, and sauté until softened and translucent. Remove from the skillet and spread them over the bottom of the tian or ovenproof dish.

Arrange overlapping layers of the tomatoes, eggplants, and zucchinis or squash on top—arrange them in lines across the dish, like fish scales. Tuck the chopped thyme between the layers and season with salt and pepper. Brush with the extra olive oil and cook in a preheated oven at 400°F for about 20 minutes.

Meanwhile, to make the topping, put the lemon zest and crushed garlic in a bowl and mix well. Stir in the bread crumbs and cheese, then sprinkle them over the top of the tian. Continue cooking for at least 30 minutes or until browned, finishing under the broiler if necessary. Serve topped with basil leaves, if using.

The colors in this casserole are equaled only by its flavor. Both are startling and gorgeous. Don't overdo the harissa—a little is enough wake you up! Let the vegetables char and acquire a bit of barbecue flavor—and don't forget the yogurt.

north african charred vegetables

3 red onions, cut into wedges

18 cherry tomatoes

1 large zucchini, cut into wedges

6 oz. small red potatoes, cut in half

2 red bell peppers, seeded and cut into strips or wedges

1 yellow bell pepper, seeded and cut into strips or wedges

2 fennel bulbs, cut into wedges

⅓ cup olive oil

6 garlic cloves, crushed to a paste

½ teaspoon harissa paste

1 teaspoon ground cumin

1 tablespoon vinegar

1 tablespoon chopped fresh mint

1 tablespoon chopped fresh cilantro

2 teaspoons sea salt

2 cups thick plain yogurt, to serve

a shallow casserole dish

serves 4–6

Set aside 1 onion and 4 cherry tomatoes. Arrange the remaining vegetables in a roasting pan, drizzle with ¼ cup of the oil, and roast in a preheated oven at 475°F or the highest oven temperature your stove has, until they begin to char, about 30 minutes.

Lower the heat to 350°F. Remove the vegetables from the oven and transfer to a shallow casserole dish.

Put the crushed garlic in a small bowl and mash in the harissa, cumin, and remaining oil. Stir in the vinegar, mint, and cilantro. Mix this in with the vegetables, tuck in the last onion and 4 cherry tomatoes, sprinkle generously with salt, and return the casserole to the oven to bake for a further 25 minutes.

If there is too much liquid, pour it off into a small saucepan, bring to a boil, and simmer until reduced and concentrated in flavor. Pour back into the casserole.

Serve with yogurt.

chickpea and tomato masala
with beans and cilantro

1 thick slice fresh ginger, chopped

2 garlic cloves, coarsely chopped

2 tablespoons safflower oil

¼ teaspoon ground turmeric

3 fresh green chiles, cut in half

1 teaspoon cumin seeds

1 onion, cut in half lengthwise, then sliced
into half-rings

8 oz. green beans, trimmed,
about 1½–2 cups

30 oz. canned chickpeas,
rinsed and drained, about 5 cups

a pinch of ground cloves

a pinch of ground cinnamon

1 teaspoon ground coriander

¼ teaspoon ground cumin

8 oz. cherry tomatoes, quartered,
about 1½ cups

sea salt and freshly ground black pepper

to serve

chopped cilantro leaves (optional)

Indian bread, such as pooris, chapatis, nan
bread, or buttered pita breads

serves 4–6

A satisfying dish with Indian flavors in which, instead of a typically smooth tomato-based sauce, cherry tomatoes are folded in at the last moment. It is based on *chole* or *channa masala*, a great Indian vegetarian dish.

Using a mortar and pestle, mash the ginger and garlic to a chunky paste. Heat the oil in a saucepan, add the turmeric, chiles, and cumin seeds, and sauté briefly. Add the onions and sauté for about 6 minutes. Add the ginger and garlic paste and sauté for 2–3 minutes more, until the onions have softened.

Add the green beans and ½ cup water, then bring to a boil. Lower the heat and cook gently for 10 minutes. Add the chickpeas, ground cloves, cinnamon, coriander, and cumin. Add salt and pepper to taste, and mix well. Cook for 9 minutes more. Gently fold in the cherry tomatoes with a wooden spoon. Turn off the heat, cover, and steam for 1–2 minutes. Sprinkle with chopped cilantro, if using, and serve with Indian breads or buttered pita breads.

pumpkin and tofu laksa

8 oz. peeled, seeded butternut squash or pumpkin, cut into ½-inch cubes

10 oz. tofu, dried with paper towels and cut into 4 triangles

3¼ cups coconut milk

¼ cup light soy sauce

2 teaspoons sugar

6 oz. rice vermicelli noodles

2½ cups bean sprouts

1 medium tomato, cut into 8 wedges

2 inches cucumber, cut into thin strips

8 sprigs of cilantro

a large handful of mint leaves

2 scallions, chopped

sea salt

sunflower oil, for sautéing

spice paste

2 garlic cloves, coarsely chopped

2 red chiles, seeded and coarsely chopped

2 inches fresh ginger root, peeled and finely grated

1 small onion

¼ teaspoon ground turmeric

2 stalks fresh lemongrass, sliced

4 fresh kaffir lime leaves, chopped

serves 4

Laksa is a Malaysian curry. It usually consists of rice noodles, crunchy raw vegetables, and fragrant herbs, bathed in a spicy coconut soup. If you can't find lemongrass or kaffir lime leaves, replace them with grated lime zest and fresh lemon juice.

To make the spice paste, put all the ingredients, plus 3 tablespoons water, in a blender or spice grinder and purée until smooth (add more water, if necessary).

Put the squash or pumpkin in a saucepan, then add salt and 2 cups water. Bring to a boil, then simmer for 10 minutes, until the cubes are tender, but still chunky. Drain, reserving the cooking liquid.

Heat 1 inch sunflower oil in a wok or skillet. Add the tofu and sauté until golden and crisp all over. Remove with a slotted spoon and drain on crumpled paper towels. Set aside.

Heat 2 tablespoons of the oil in a saucepan, add the spice paste, and sauté for 2 minutes to release the aromas. Add the coconut milk, fried tofu, soy sauce, and sugar. Add the reserved pumpkin liquid. Bring to a boil, then simmer for 10 minutes.

Meanwhile, put the noodles in a bowl, cover with boiling water, and let soak for 5 minutes. Drain, and divide between 4 warmed bowls.

Add the bean sprouts, tomato, and cooked squash or pumpkin. Lay a piece of sautéed tofu in each bowl. Ladle the hot coconut soup over them, top with the cucumber, cilantro, mint, and scallions, then serve.

roasted teriyaki tofu steaks

1 lb. fresh firm tofu, cut into 4 pieces

4 fresh or dried shiitake mushrooms (optional)

8 oz. fresh or dried egg noodles

teriyaki marinade

½ cup dark soy sauce

½ cup mirin (Japanese sweet rice wine)

½ cup sake

1 tablespoon sugar

glazed green vegetables

2 tablespoons sunflower oil

2 garlic cloves, thinly sliced

1 cup broccoli florets or chopped broccoli rabe

1 leek, white and light-green parts, thinly sliced

8 oz. baby bok choy, quartered lengthwise, or 2 cups chopped spinach leaves

1 fennel bulb, trimmed and thinly sliced

2 teaspoons cornstarch mixed with ¼ cup cold water

to serve

2 scallions, thinly sliced diagonally

1 tablespoon sesame seeds, toasted in a dry skillet until golden-brown

a baking dish, lightly oiled

serves 4

Dark soy sauce, sweet mirin, and dry sake give teriyaki its unique flavors. You can buy it ready-made, but this only faintly resembles the real thing, so make your own—it's easy.

To make the marinade, put the soy sauce, mirin, sake, and sugar in a large skillet and heat, stirring until the sugar has dissolved. Add the tofu and mushrooms, if using. Simmer gently for about 15 minutes, turning the tofu over halfway through cooking.

Transfer the tofu steaks to a lightly oiled baking dish or roasting pan. Spoon a little sauce on top and roast in a preheated oven at 425°F for 10 minutes. Keep them warm in a low oven. Using a slotted spoon, remove the mushrooms from the remaining sauce, squeeze dry, and slice thinly. Reserve the sauce.

To make the glazed vegetables, heat a wok until hot, then add the oil. Add the garlic, broccoli, leek, and sliced mushrooms, and stir-fry for 2 minutes. Add the bok choy or spinach, and fennel. Stir-fry for 2 minutes. Add the reserved sauce and ¼ cup water, stir, cover, and cook for 2 minutes. Push the vegetables to the back of the wok, add the cornstarch mixture to the bubbling juices, and stir until thickened. Mix the vegetables into the sauce. Cook the noodles according to the package instructions, then drain.

To serve, put a nest of noodles on warmed plates and pile on the vegetables. Turn the tofu steaks over and put shiny side up on top of the vegetables. Sprinkle with the scallions and toasted sesame seeds.

This popular Thai classic is super-quick to make and always gets rave reviews.

green thai vegetable curry

3 tablespoons green Thai curry paste

1¼ cups canned coconut milk

1¼ cups vegetable stock

1 large potato, peeled and cut into 1-inch pieces

8 oz. broccoli florets, about 3–4 cups

8 oz. cauliflower florets, about 3–4 cups

1 cup frozen peas

1 cup sugar snap peas, cut in half lengthwise

to serve

1 lime, cut into wedges

cooked Thai fragrant rice

serves 4

To cook the Thai fragrant rice, rinse to remove the starch, put in a large saucepan, and add cold water to 1 inch above the rice level. Cover with a lid and bring to a boil, reduce the heat, and simmer until the water is absorbed, about 5 minutes. Remove the pan from the heat and let stand, with the lid on, for about 10 minutes until cooked.

Meanwhile, put the curry paste in a large wok, heat, and cook for 2 minutes, stirring. Add the coconut milk, stock, and potato. Bring to a boil, reduce the heat, and simmer for 5 minutes. Add the broccoli and cauliflower florets, stalk end down, cover with a lid, and simmer for 4 minutes. Add the peas and sugar snap peas and cook for a further 2 minutes, until all the vegetables are tender.

Ladle the curry into 4 bowls and serve with lime wedges and the Thai fragrant rice.

Roquefort is a salty French blue cheese that's made with ewes' milk, but you could substitute any good-quality blue cheese when making this recipe.

roquefort tart
with walnut and toasted garlic dressing

1 recipe Pâte Brisée dough (page 235)

8 oz. cream cheese, about 1 cup

⅔ cup sour cream or crème fraîche

3 large eggs, beaten

7 oz. Roquefort cheese or other good blue cheese, about 1½–2 cups

freshly grated nutmeg, to taste

3 tablespoons chopped fresh chives

freshly ground black pepper

walnut and toasted garlic dressing

3 garlic cloves

2 tablespoons olive oil

3 oz. walnut halves, about ¾ cup

1 tablespoon walnut oil

3 tablespoons chopped fresh parsley

a removable-bottomed tart pan, 10 inches diameter

foil or baking parchment and baking beans

serves 6

Bring the dough to room temperature. Preheat the oven to 400°F.

Roll out the dough thinly on a lightly floured counter, then use to line the tart pan. Prick the bottom, chill or freeze for 15 minutes, then bake blind following the method on page 203.

To make the filling, put the cream cheese in a bowl and beat until softened. Beat in the cream or crème fraîche and the eggs. Crumble in the blue cheese and mix gently. Season with lots of black pepper and nutmeg. The cheese is salty, so you won't have to add extra salt. Stir in the chives, and set aside.

Let the pie crust cool slightly and lower the oven temperature to 375°F. Pour the filling into the crust and bake for 30–35 minutes or until the filling is puffed and golden brown.

Meanwhile, to make the walnut and garlic dressing, slice the garlic into the thinnest of slivers. Heat the olive oil in a skillet and add the garlic and walnuts. Stir-fry until the garlic is golden and the walnuts browned. Stir in the walnut oil and parsley.

Serve the tart warm or at room temperature, with the warm walnut and garlic dressing to pour over the tart.

Perfect for a summer lunch, this Mediterranean recipe and simple char-grilling technique bring out the best in zucchini. They cook to a sensuous texture and absorb the contrasting flavors of the tangy vinegar and fragrant mint.

minted grilled zucchini

4 medium zucchinis, about 2 lb.

2 tablespoons olive oil

4 teaspoons white wine vinegar

a handful of mint leaves, torn

sea salt and freshly ground black pepper

serves 4

Trim and discard the ends off the zucchinis, then cut the vegetable lengthwise into ribbon-like slices and put in a bowl. Drizzle with the olive oil and, using your hands, gently toss the slices until well coated.

Heat a stove-top grill pan or nonstick skillet until very hot. Add the zucchini ribbons (in batches, if necessary) and cook until softened and marked with black stripes on both sides (if using a grill pan). Transfer to a shallow dish and drizzle with the vinegar while they are still warm. Sprinkle with salt and let cool.

Pile the zucchini ribbons in a serving bowl, sprinkle with the mint and lots of pepper. Serve.

"Greens"—used loosely to describe any leafy green vegetable—include Swiss chard, bok choy, beet greens, spinach, and more. Many need only brief steaming or stir-frying to retain color, nutrients, and flavor. Remove any tough stalks before you start cooking.

chile greens with garlic crisps

1 lb. greens (see introduction right)

2 tablespoons olive oil

4 garlic cloves, sliced

1 red serrano chile, seeded and thinly sliced

salt and freshly ground black pepper

serves 4

Coarsely chop the greens, but if using bok choy, cut lengthwise into wedges. Gently heat the olive oil in a large saucepan. Add the garlic, sauté until golden and crisp, about 2–3 minutes, then remove and set aside. Add the chile to the infused oil in the pan and cook for 1 minute. Tip in the greens—they will splutter, so stand back. Add salt and pepper and mix well. Cover and cook, turning the greens occasionally using tongs, until tender: spring greens will take 5 minutes; Swiss chard, bok choy, and beet greens, about 3 minutes; and spinach about 1–2 minutes.

Transfer to a warmed serving dish, top with the garlic crisps, and serve immediately.

This easy, delicious dish can be used in lots of ways—piled on top of pizza, as an appetizer, mixed with pasta, or as a vegetable accompaniment to an entrée.

wilted spinach
with garlic, pine nuts, and raisins

2 tablespoons extra virgin olive oil

3 tablespoons pine nuts

2 garlic cloves, crushed

6 canned anchovy fillets, chopped

18 oz. well-washed spinach, water still clinging, about 5 cups

3 tablespoons seedless raisins

sea salt and cracked black pepper, to serve

serves 4

Heat the oil in a skillet. Add the pine nuts, stir-fry for about 1 minute until golden, then remove quickly with a slotted spoon, or drain through a strainer, reserving the oil and returning it to the skillet.

Add the garlic and anchovies to the skillet and mash them together over a medium heat until aromatic, then add the wet spinach and raisins. Toss carefully with tongs or wooden spoons until evenly distributed. Cover the skillet and cook over medium heat for 2–3 minutes, stirring halfway through.

Uncover the skillet, sprinkle with the pine nuts, and toss well until gleaming. Serve hot or warm, with small dishes of salt and cracked black pepper.

provençal roasted vegetables

Preparation is kept to a minimum and the result is a thing of beauty. Make sure you provide a side plate to put the bits on as people pluck their way through the sweet, juicy vegetables

1 medium eggplant

2 medium zucchinis

4 red onions, unpeeled

2 red serrano chiles

1 whole head of garlic, unpeeled

4 plum tomatoes or 16 cherry tomatoes, preferably "on the vine"

4 sprigs of rosemary

¾ cup olive oil

freshly squeezed juice of ½ lemon

sea salt and freshly ground black pepper

serves 4

Cut the eggplant lengthwise into quarters and score the flesh with a crisscross pattern. Slice the zucchini in half lengthwise. Cut a thin slice off the bottom of the onions and cut a cross in the top. Split the chiles in half. Leave the garlic whole.

Put all the vegetables, except the tomatoes, cut side up in a roasting pan or dish. Tuck the rosemary and chiles into the onions. Reserve 2 tablespoons of oil and brush the remainder all over the vegetables. Drizzle with the lemon juice and sprinkle with salt and pepper.

Roast in a preheated oven at 400°F for 30 minutes, then brush the tomatoes with the remaining oil and put them on top of the half-roasted vegetables. Cook for 15-20 minutes, until the vegetables are golden and the tomatoes have split. If using cherry tomatoes, add them after the vegetables have cooked for 40 minutes, and roast for 5-10 minutes more. Serve.

Potatoes love to be roasted. These zesty little spuds have a crisp tangy exterior and are fluffy inside. Serve with steamed greens or roasted vegetables.

lemon-roasted new potatoes

2 lb. baby new potatoes, scrubbed

¼ cup olive oil

2 unwaxed lemons, grated zest of both, and juice of 1

1 teaspoon sugar

sea salt and freshly ground black pepper

serves 4

Cook the potatoes in salted boiling water for 5 minutes, drain, then transfer to a roasting pan.

Put the olive oil, lemon zest and juice, sugar, salt, and pepper in a bowl and whisk. Pour over the potatoes and toss well to coat.

Roast in a preheated oven at 375°F for 20–30 minutes, turning and basting the potatoes frequently with the pan juices, until golden and tender.

The ultimate comfort food, creamy mashed potatoes make the perfect partner for good-quality broiled sausages (page 163) or any other broiled meat. Choose large "old" potatoes—the sort that become fluffy when mashed. When boiling potatoes, it's always important to add salt before cooking.

classic creamy mashed potatoes

2 lb. large "old" potatoes, such as baking potatoes, peeled and cut into 2-inch cubes

about ⅔ cup milk, preferably hot

3 tablespoons butter

sea salt and freshly ground black pepper

serves 4

Put the potatoes in a large saucepan. Add cold water to cover and a pinch of salt. Bring to a boil, reduce the heat, cover with a lid, and simmer for 15–20 minutes, until tender when pierced with a knife. Drain and return the potatoes to the pan.

Return the saucepan to the heat and mash the potatoes with a fork or potato masher for 30 seconds—this will steam off any excess water. Stir in the milk and butter with a spoon. Mash until smooth, adding extra milk if needed, and salt and pepper to taste. Serve immediately, in a serving bowl or right onto plates.

fish & seafood

steamed mussels
with garlic and vermouth in a foil package

The vermouth turns to steam in these package of foil and cooks the mussels in a delicious scented vapor. Let guests open their own packages and watch their delight as they breathe in the heavenly aroma.

2 lb. mussels, in their shells

4 tablespoons butter

⅔ cup dry vermouth

2 garlic cloves, crushed

to serve

crusty bread

a bunch of flat-leaf parsley, coarsely chopped (optional)

4 pieces of foil, about 24 x 12 inches

1 baking tray

serves 4

Scrub the mussels clean and rinse them in several changes of cold water to remove grit. Pull off the beards or seaweed-like threads and discard any mussels that are cracked or that don't close when tapped against the kitchen counter—these are dead and not edible.

Fold the pieces of foil in half lengthwise and divide the butter, vermouth, garlic, and mussels between them. Bring the corners of each piece together to close the package, leaving a little space in each one so the mussels with have room to open. Pinch the edges of the packages together to seal.

Put the packages on a baking tray and cook in a preheated oven at 400°F for 10-12 minutes or until all the mussels have opened—check one of the packages to see.

Put the packages on warmed plates and serve with crusty bread to mop up the delicious juices. If you like, put coarsely chopped parsley in a bowl and serve separately for people to sprinkle over their mussels when they open the packages.

seared scallops
with crushed potatoes

12 large sea scallops
1 tablespoon extra virgin olive oil
sea salt and freshly ground black pepper

crushed potatoes

1 lb. new potatoes, peeled
1 tablespoon extra virgin olive oil
¼ cup pitted black olives, chopped
1 tablespoon chopped fresh flat-leaf parsley
a few drops of truffle oil (optional)
sea salt and freshly ground black pepper

serves 4

With their sweet flesh and subtle hint of the sea, scallops are a real treat. Truffle oil, though expensive, is used sparingly and transforms this dish into something special. If you don't have any truffle oil, use a flavored oil of your choice.

Cook the potatoes in a saucepan of lightly salted, boiling water until just tender. Drain well and return to the pan. Lightly crush them with a fork, leaving them still a little chunky. Add the olive oil, olives, parsley, and a few drops of truffle oil, if using. Season with salt and pepper and stir well.

Put the scallops in a bowl, add the olive oil, salt, and pepper. Toss to coat. Sear the scallops on a preheated stove-top grill pan for 1 minute on each side (don't overcook or they will be tough). Remove to a plate and let them rest briefly.

Put a pile of crushed potatoes onto each plate, lay the scallops on top, and sprinkle with a few extra drops of truffle oil, if using.

Fast stir-frying is great for seafood, which mustn't be overcooked. It's also great for easy entertaining. You can make the salsa and the prawn mixture ahead of time, then all you need are a few minutes to fry the prawns and serve.

hot wok chile shrimp

1 red serrano chile

1 lb. peeled, uncooked shrimp, with tails intact

grated zest and freshly squeezed juice of 1 unwaxed lime

1 garlic clove, chopped

2 tablespoons canola or safflower oil

a pinch of sugar

cucumber cilantro salsa

½ cucumber, peeled

a bunch of cilantro

1 tablespoon rice vinegar

1 teaspoon sugar

sea salt and freshly ground black pepper

serves 4

To prepare the chile, cut it in half lengthwise, then scrape out and discard the seeds. Cut each half lengthwise into thin strips. Cut the strips crosswise into very fine dice. Put the shrimp in a bowl and add the chile, lime zest and juice, garlic, 1 tablespoon of the oil, and the sugar. Using a potato peeler, remove the peel from the cucumber.

To make the cilantro salsa, cut the peeled cucumber into slices lengthwise, then stack the slices and cut them into strips. Cut the strips crosswise into dice. Coarsely chop the cilantro. Put the cucumber and cilantro in a second bowl, add the rice vinegar and sugar, then mix, adding salt and pepper to taste.

Heat the remaining oil in a wok over high heat and add half the shrimp mixture. Stir-fry for 1–2 minutes until pink and cooked. Keep them warm in a very low oven while you stir-fry the remaining shrimp. When cooked, divide the shrimp between 4 plates and serve the cucumber cilantro salsa in bowls alongside.

2 large eggs

⅔ cup ice-cold sparkling water

¾ cup all-purpose flour

⅓ cup cornstarch

3 tablespoons finely chopped chives

1 lb. salmon fillet, sliced crosswise into 16 finger-size strips

canola or safflower oil, for frying

sea salt

chile sauce

⅓ cup sesame seeds, toasted

3 red serrano chiles, finely chopped

2 tablespoons dark soy sauce

1 tablespoon white wine vinegar

1 tablespoon honey

serves 4

Tempura batter shouldn't be smooth, so mix it very briefly, using chopsticks rather than a fork. Make the batter just before you use it.

salmon tempura

To make the sauce, put the sesame seeds and chiles in a bowl and add the soy sauce. Add the vinegar and honey. Stir.

To make the batter, crack the eggs into a bowl. Pour in the sparkling water and mix quickly. Add the flours and stir briefly with chopsticks. Don't overmix—the batter should have lumps. Add the chives and stir briefly.

Pour the oil into a deep-fryer, saucepan, or wok and heat. To test the heat of the oil, add a cube of white bread. If it browns in 20 seconds, the oil is ready for cooking. If you have a cooking thermometer, it should read 385°F.

Dip the salmon pieces into the batter. Add the pieces to the pan, 3 at a time, and fry, in batches, for 2–3 minutes until golden. Remove from the oil, drain on paper towels and sprinkle with salt. Serve immediately with the chile sauce.

roasted salmon
wrapped in prosciutto

4 thin slices Fontina cheese, rind removed

4 salmon fillets, 8 oz. each, skinned

4 bay leaves

8 thin slices prosciutto

sea salt and freshly ground black pepper

zucchini ribbons and pasta

8 oz. dried pasta

8 oz. zucchini, very thinly sliced lengthwise

finely grated zest and freshly squeezed juice of 1 unwaxed lemon

2 tablespoons extra virgin olive oil

a bunch of chives, finely chopped

a baking tray, lightly oiled

serves 4

What makes this dish such a joy is that you will have no last-minute dramas with the fish falling to pieces, because the prosciutto not only adds flavor and crispness, it also wraps around the salmon and makes it easier to handle.

Trim the Fontina slices to fit on top of the salmon fillets. Put a bay leaf on each fillet, then a slice of the Fontina. Wrap 2 slices of prosciutto around each piece of salmon, so that it is completely covered.

Transfer to the baking tray and cook in a preheated oven at 400°F for about 10–15 minutes, depending on the thickness of the salmon fillets.

Meanwhile, cook the pasta in a large saucepan of boiling, salted water until al dente, or according to the directions on the package. Add the zucchini slices to the pasta for the final 3 minutes of cooking.

Put the lemon zest and juice in a bowl, add the oil, and mix. Add the chives, salt, and pepper. Drain the pasta and zucchini and return them to the pan. Add the lemon juice mixture and toss well to coat. Serve with the roasted salmon.

seared swordfish

with avocado and salsa

2 tablespoons olive oil

grated zest and juice of 2 unwaxed limes

4 swordfish steaks

freshly ground black pepper

2 large, just-ripe avocados, cut in half, pitted, peeled, and sliced

salsa

1 small red onion, chopped

1 red chile, seeded and very finely chopped

1 large ripe tomato, cut in half, seeded, and chopped

3 tablespoons extra virgin olive oil

grated zest and juice of 1 unwaxed lime

to serve

a bunch of cilantro, chopped

1 lime, cut into wedges

serves 4

Like tuna, swordfish is perfect for the grill—its texture is quite meat-like, so it doesn't flake or fall apart.

Put the oil, lime zest, and juice in a small bowl and beat well. Add plenty of black pepper. Put the swordfish steaks in a shallow dish and pour the oil and lime mixture over them, making sure the fish is coated on all sides. Cover and refrigerate for up to 1 hour.

Meanwhile, to make the salsa, put the onion, chile, tomato, oil, lime zest, and juice in a bowl. Mix gently, then cover and refrigerate.

Heat a stove-top grill pan to hot and cook the fish for 2–3 minutes on each side, until just cooked through. Serve the avocado slices and fish on 4 plates, spoon the salsa over them, sprinkle with cilantro, and serve with lime wedges.

peppered tuna steak
with salsa rossa

You can make the salsa rossa in advance—it can be stored in the refrigerator for up to three days—leaving you very little to do when your guests arrive.

⅓ cup mixed peppercorns, coarsely crushed

6 tuna steaks, 8 oz. each

1 tablespoon extra virgin olive oil

salad greens, to serve

salsa rossa

1 large red bell pepper

1 tablespoon extra virgin olive oil

2 garlic cloves, crushed

2 large ripe tomatoes, peeled and coarsely chopped

a small pinch of hot red pepper flakes

1 tablespoon dried oregano

1 tablespoon red wine vinegar

sea salt and freshly ground black pepper

serves 6

To make the salsa rossa, broil the pepper until charred all over, then put into a plastic bag and let cool. Remove and discard the skin and seeds, reserving any juices, then chop the flesh.

Put the oil in a skillet, heat gently, then add the garlic, and sauté for 3 minutes. Add the tomatoes, pepper flakes, and oregano, and simmer gently for 15 minutes. Stir in the peppers and the vinegar, and simmer for a further 5 minutes to evaporate any excess liquid.

Transfer to a blender and purée until fairly smooth. Add salt and pepper to taste, and let cool. It may be stored in a screw-top jar in the refrigerator for up to 3 days.

Put the crushed peppercorns on a large plate. Brush the tuna steaks with oil, then press the crushed peppercorns into the surface. Preheat a stove-top grill pan or outdoor grill until hot, add the tuna, and cook for 1 minute on each side. Wrap loosely in foil and let rest for 5 minutes before serving with the salsa rossa and a salad of mixed greens.

Roasted vegetables make a delicious base for broiled fish in this recipe. You can roast the fish too—just remember it will take a very short time, so cook it just until the flesh turns opaque (white all the way through).

saffron fish roast

2 red onions, cut into wedges

2 red bell peppers, cut in half, seeded, and each half cut into 3

1 lb. new potatoes

1 tablespoon olive oil

8 oz. baby plum tomatoes

1 lb. thick, skinless cod fillet, cut into 4 chunks

1 lb. thick, skinless salmon fillet, cut into 4 slices

½ teaspoon sea salt

freshly ground black pepper

1 lemon, cut into wedges, to serve

marinade

a pinch of saffron threads

¼ cup finely chopped flat-leaf parsley

2 tablespoons extra virgin olive oil

serves 4

Put the saffron in a small bowl, add 3 tablespoons boiling water, and set aside to soak.

Put the onions, bell peppers, and potatoes in a large roasting pan. Add the olive oil, and salt and pepper to taste, and mix well. Roast in a preheated oven at 400°F for about 45 minutes, until the vegetables are cooked and slightly charred. Add the tomatoes to the pan and roast for a further 5 minutes.

Meanwhile, put the saffron and its soaking water in a large bowl, add the parsley and oil, along with black pepper to taste, and mix. Put the fish in a shallow dish and pour the marinade over it. Cover, and refrigerate until needed.

Preheat the broiler to medium heat. Remove the fish from its marinade and discard the marinade. Put the fish on top of the vegetables in the roasting pan. Sprinkle with the sea salt, and cook under the broiler for 10–12 minutes, until the fish is just cooked through.

Divide the fish and vegetables between 4 plates, and serve with the lemon wedges.

mediterranean fish stew

Shrimp shells are full of flavor, and this will seep into the sauce, contributing to its richness. Eat this dish with your fingers and mop up with plenty of crusty fresh bread.

12 mussels

1 large fennel bulb, with leafy tops

2 tablespoons olive oil

2 garlic cloves, crushed

¾ cup dry white wine

1¼ cups fish stock

29 oz. canned chopped tomatoes, about 3 cups

a pinch of sugar

1 cup cherry tomatoes, cut in half, about 1½ cups

1 lb. monkfish fillet, cut into 1½-inch chunks

12 large, unpeeled, raw shrimp, heads removed

sea salt and freshly ground black pepper

extra virgin olive oil, to serve

serves 4

Scrub the mussels clean and rinse them in several changes of cold water to remove grit. Pull off the beards or seaweed-like threads, and discard any mussels that are cracked or that don't close when tapped against the countertop—these are dead and not edible.

Remove the leafy tops from the fennel bulb, chop them coarsely, and set aside. Cut the bulb into quarters, remove and discard the core, then finely chop the bulb.

Heat the oil in a large saucepan or wok. Add the fennel bulb and sauté for 5 minutes. Add the garlic and sauté for a further 1 minute. Add the wine, stock, canned tomatoes, and sugar, and stir well. Bring to a boil, reduce the heat, then simmer for 5 minutes. Add the cherry tomatoes and cook for a further 5 minutes. Add plenty of salt and pepper.

Add the monkfish and return to simmering. Stir in the mussels and shrimp, cover, and cook for about 5 minutes, or until the mussels have opened and the fish is cooked.

Ladle the stew into deep plates or bowls. Sprinkle with the fennel tops and olive oil, and serve.

There may seem to be a lot of mustard in this sauce, but it loses its heat when cooked and you are left with a delicious flavor which no one can quite place once the poaching liquid has been added.

traditional fish pie

2 cups milk

1½ lb. smoked or fresh haddock, skinned

2⅓ sticks unsalted butter

1 tablespoon dry mustard powder

¼ cup all-purpose flour

2 hard-cooked eggs, peeled and quartered

2 lb. baking potatoes

sea salt and freshly ground black pepper

a shallow baking dish or casserole dish

serves 4

Put the milk in a wide saucepan, heat just to boiling point, then add the fish. Turn off the heat and let the fish poach until opaque. Do not overcook.

Meanwhile, melt 1 stick of the butter in another saucepan, then stir in the mustard and flour. Remove from the heat and strain the poaching liquid into the pan.

Arrange the fish and eggs in a shallow baking or casserole dish.

Return the pan to the heat and, whisking vigorously to smooth out any lumps, bring the mixture to a boil. Season with salt and pepper, if necessary. (Take care with the salt: if you are using smoked fish, it may be salty enough.) Pour the sauce into the casserole dish and mix carefully with the fish and eggs.

Cook the potatoes in boiling salted water until soft, then drain. Return to the pan. Melt the remaining 1⅓ sticks butter in a small saucepan. Reserve ¼ cup of this butter and stir the remainder into the potatoes. Mash well, and season with salt and pepper. Spoon the potatoes carefully over the fish mixture, brush generously with the reserved butter, and transfer to a preheated oven at 400°F for 20 minutes, or until nicely browned.

chicken
& duck

pan-fried chicken
with creamy beans and leeks

This is a great supper dish for weekday entertaining—simple and quick. The combination of beans and leeks, which is also very good with lamb, makes for a satisfying meal, though if you want something lighter you could serve a simple green salad instead.

4 boneless chicken breasts

2 tablespoons unsalted butter

1 tablespoon extra virgin olive oil

sea salt and freshly ground black pepper

watercress or spinach salad, to serve

mustard and tarragon butter

2 tablespoons chopped fresh
tarragon leaves

1 tablespoon whole grain mustard

1¼ sticks unsalted butter, softened

creamy beans with leeks

4 tablespoons unsalted butter

2 leeks, finely chopped

1 garlic clove, crushed

2 teaspoons chopped fresh rosemary

28 oz. canned flageolet beans, about
5 cups, rinsed and drained

1¼ cups vegetable stock

¼ cup heavy cream

serves 4

To make the mustard and tarragon butter, beat the tarragon leaves and mustard into the butter. Roll into a small log, wrap in plastic wrap, and freeze until needed.

To cook the beans and leeks, melt the butter in a saucepan, add the leeks, garlic, and rosemary, and sauté gently for 5 minutes, until softened but not golden. Add the beans, stir once, then pour in the stock. Bring to a boil, cover, and simmer for 15 minutes. Remove the lid, stir in the cream, and add salt and pepper to taste. Simmer, uncovered, for a further 5 minutes, until the sauce has thickened. Set aside.

Season the chicken with salt and pepper. Heat the butter and oil in a skillet, and as soon as the butter stops foaming, cook the chicken, skin side down, for 4 minutes. Turn it over and cook for a further 4 minutes.

Top each breast with a couple of slices of the mustard and tarragon butter, and let rest for 2–3 minutes in a low oven. Serve with the beans and leeks and a watercress salad.

These mini chickens can be roasted in about forty minutes. To make sure they are cooked through, push a skewer into the leg meat right down to the bone. If the juices run clear, the birds are cooked. If not, return them to the oven for a little longer.

garlic-roasted cornish hens

2 whole heads of garlic, cloves separated but unpeeled

2 Cornish hens

½ unwaxed lemon

4 sprigs of thyme

4 tablespoons unsalted butter, softened

½ cup white wine

1¼ cups chicken stock

1 tablespoon all-purpose flour

sea salt and freshly ground black pepper

serves 4

Boil the garlic cloves in a saucepan of lightly salted water for 15 minutes, drain, and pat dry (this can be done ahead of time).

Meanwhile, wash the hens, pat them dry, and rub all over with the cut lemon. Chop the lemon into small chunks and put them and the thyme in the birds' body cavities. Season well with salt and pepper and rub the birds all over with 3 tablespoons of the butter.

Put 1 garlic clove in each bird, then put the rest of the garlic in a large roasting pan. Sit the hens on top and roast in a preheated oven at 400°F for 40 minutes. Transfer the hens and garlic cloves to a large plate, wrap loosely in aluminum foil, and let rest for 10 minutes.

Meanwhile, to make a gravy, spoon off any excess fat from the roasting pan and discard. Add the wine to the juices in the roasting pan, place over a burner, bring to a boil, and scrape any sediments into the wine. Boil until reduced by two-thirds. Add the stock and boil for 5 minutes, or until reduced by half. Put the remaining butter and the flour in a bowl and beat until smooth. Gradually beat into the gravy, stirring over gentle heat until thickened.

Serve the Cornish hens with the garlic and gravy.

coq au vin

This is France's most famous stew. To be authentic, it should contain mushrooms, diced bacon, and caramelized baby onions.

1 large chicken, preferably free-range or
corn-fed, cut into serving pieces

leaves from 1 sprig of thyme,
finely chopped

4 tablespoons butter

⅓ cup brandy

1 bottle rich red wine, 750 ml

3 cups chicken stock

4 tomatoes, peeled and seeded,
or 2 teaspoons tomato paste

2 garlic cloves, crushed

1 bay leaf

sea salt and freshly ground black pepper

roux

4 tablespoons butter

2 tablespoons all-purpose flour

to serve

4 oz. thick-cut bacon, diced

1¼ sticks butter

1 cup button mushrooms, sliced

12 baby onions

a large flameproof casserole dish

serves 4

Season the chicken pieces with salt and pepper and sprinkle with the thyme. Put the butter in a large, flameproof casserole dish and heat on the stove until it begins to brown. Add the chicken to the casserole dish and sauté, skin side down, until golden brown.

Remove the casserole dish from the heat, pour the brandy into it, and ignite it if you wish—otherwise let it boil away so the alcohol evaporates. Using tongs or a slotted spoon, remove the chicken to a plate and keep it warm in a low oven. Pour the wine into the casserole dish, bring to a boil, and reduce to about 3–4 tablespoons. Add the tomatoes or paste, garlic, and bay leaf, and mix.

To make the roux, heat the butter in a small skillet, add the flour, and cook, stirring, until the mixture is a pale brown. Stir it into the wine mixture.

Reserve 1 cup of the stock, stir the remainder into the casserole, and bring to a boil. Add the chicken pieces and any juices that have run onto the plate. Season to taste with salt and pepper, cover with a lid, and cook in a preheated oven at 350°F for 40 minutes, or until the chicken juices run clear when pricked with a fork. Meanwhile, bring a saucepan of water to a boil, add the bacon, boil for 1 minute, then drain. Add the bacon to the casserole dish halfway through the cooking time.

Put 6 tablespoons of the serving butter in a small skillet, add the mushrooms, and sauté for 5 minutes. Transfer to the casserole dish for the last 5 minutes of cooking time. Add the remaining butter to the skillet, add the onions, and sauté until browned, about 5 minutes. Add the reserved 1 cup chicken stock, bring to a boil, and simmer until tender and the stock has been absorbed, about 10 minutes.

Serve on warmed plates, topping each chicken piece with a share of the mushrooms, bacon, and golden onions.

There won't be many people who don't appreciate this dish. Stir-fried also effectively means "steam-stirred," because the vegetables are mostly cooked in the aromatic steam. Use a sweet chile sauce, not a fiery Southeast Asian version.

stir-fried chicken with greens

2 tablespoons peanut oil

3 large, skinless, boneless chicken breasts cut into 2-inch strips or cubes, about 1 lb.

2 inches fresh ginger root, shredded

2 garlic cloves, sliced

8 oz. broccoli, broken into tiny florets, about 3–4 cups

8 scallions, cut in half crosswise

8 oz. green beans, cut in half and blanched in boiling salted water, about 1½ cups

1 red or yellow bell pepper, seeded and cut into strips

⅓ cup chicken stock or water

2 tablespoons sweet chile sauce

1 tablespoon light soy sauce

2 oz. snow peas, trimmed and washed

2 oz. sugar snap peas, trimmed and washed

4 oz. baby bok choy leaves, trimmed and washed

noodles or rice, to serve

serves 4

To blanch the beans, bring a saucepan of water to a boil, add the beans, and boil for 2–3 minutes, until they turn bright green. Drain, run under cold water, and drain again.

Put the oil in a wok and heat until very hot but not smoking. Alternatively, use a large, preferably nonstick, skillet. Add the chicken and stir-fry over high heat for 2 minutes, then add the ginger and garlic and stir-fry for a further 2 minutes.

Add the broccoli, scallions, green beans, sliced bell pepper, and chicken stock or water. Cover and cook for a further 2–3 minutes. Stir in the chile sauce and soy sauce. Toss the still-wet snow peas, sugar snap peas, and bok choy leaves on top. Cover and cook for 1–2 minutes.

Toss, then serve while the tastes and colors are still vivid and the textures crisp. Accompany with noodles or rice.

korean chicken

4 lb. chicken pieces, trimmed

¼ cup sesame oil

½ cup light soy sauce

4 garlic cloves, very finely chopped

1 teaspoon chili powder

5 scallions, very finely chopped

freshly ground black pepper

to serve

1 lb. dried egg noodles

1 teaspoon black sesame seeds
(optional)

a shallow ovenproof dish

serves 8

This traditional Korean dish, which looks and tastes great, is so simple to make. You will need to marinate the chicken the night before, but then you just transfer it from the fridge to the oven when you are ready to cook.

Put the chicken in an ovenproof dish, add the sesame oil, soy sauce, garlic, chili powder, scallions, and black pepper to taste. Mix well, cover, and chill overnight in the refrigerator.

Uncover the chicken and transfer to a preheated oven at 350°F for 30 minutes. Reduce to 275°F and cook for a further 40 minutes. Meanwhile, cook the noodles according to the directions on the package. Drain, then serve the chicken and noodles, sprinkled with the sesame seeds, if using.

hot chicken tikka platter
with yogurt

3 boneless, skinless chicken breasts, cut into strips

freshly squeezed juice of 1 lemon

¼ cup tikka or mild curry paste

2 garlic cloves, crushed

8 oz. green beans, about 1½ cups

1 tablespoon oil

1 cup baby spinach leaves

freshly ground black pepper

to serve

a bunch of cilantro, coarsely chopped (optional)

¾ cup plain yogurt

serves 4

Your friends will be most impressed when you serve up your own version of this popular Indian dish.

Put the chicken strips in a large bowl and sprinkle with the lemon juice. Add the curry paste and garlic and mix well. (If time allows, marinate in the refrigerator for 30 minutes.)

Heat a large wok or skillet. Add the chicken with its marinade and cook for about 5–7 minutes, until the chicken is opaque and cooked all the way through. Add black pepper to taste.

Meanwhile, to blanch the beans, bring a saucepan of water to a boil, add the beans, and boil for 2–3 minutes, until they turn bright green. Drain, run under cold water, and drain again. Heat a second wok or large skillet. Add the oil and, when hot, add the drained beans. Remove from the heat, and add the spinach leaves. Toss to mix.

To serve, pile the spinach and beans in the center of a large serving dish. Top with the hot chicken, sprinkle with cilantro, if using, and serve with yogurt.

Panini is the Italian word for little sandwiches, usually toasted. Here, instead of bread, try toasting (or grilling) chicken breast fillets stuffed with basil and mozzarella—melted, gooey, and delicious!

chicken "panini"
with mozzarella

8 oz. mozzarella cheese

4 large, skinless, boneless chicken breasts

8 large basil leaves

2 garlic cloves, thinly sliced

1 tablespoon olive oil

sea salt and freshly ground black pepper

to serve

salsa rossa (page 125)

basil leaves

serves 4

Cut the mozzarella into 8 thick slices and set aside.

Put the chicken breasts onto a cutting board and, using a sharp knife, cut horizontally into the thickness without cutting all the way through. Open out flat and season the insides with a little salt and pepper.

Put 2 basil leaves, a few garlic slices, and 2 slices of cheese into each breast, then close it up, pressing firmly together. Secure with toothpicks.

Brush the chicken breast pockets with a little oil and cook on a preheated outdoor grill or stove-top grill pan for about 8 minutes on each side, until the cheese is beginning to ooze at the sides and the chicken is cooked.

Serve hot with the salsa rossa and sprinkled with a few basil leaves.

honeyed duck
with mango salsa

4 small to medium duck breasts,
with skin on

1 tablespoon soy sauce

1 tablespoon honey

sea salt

mango salsa

1 large ripe mango

1 orange bell pepper, cut in half,
seeded, and diced

6 scallions, thinly sliced

2 tablespoons olive oil

grated zest and freshly squeezed juice
of 1 unwaxed orange

freshly squeezed juice of 1 lime

4 sprigs of cilantro

serves 4

Duck always works well with fruit—this recipe is also good with nectarines. Pricking the duck skin stops it shrinking as it cooks, while the honey-soy mixture produces a delicious, crackly skin.

Cut the sides off the mango in 4 slabs, from top to bottom, and discard the seed and surrounding flesh. With a small, sharp knife, cut a crisscross pattern into the flesh of each piece, down to the skin. Push the skin with your thumbs to invert it, and scrape off the cubes of flesh with a knife.

Put the mango in a bowl and add the remaining salsa ingredients. Set aside to develop the flavors. Meanwhile, preheat the oven to 450°F.

Prick the duck skin all over with a fork and rub with a little salt. Transfer the duck breasts to a wire rack set over a roasting pan (this will let the excess fat drip away).

Put the soy sauce and honey into a small bowl and mix well. Spread the mixture over the duck skin. Transfer to the oven and roast for 15–20 minutes, until the duck is just cooked but still pink in the middle, and the skin is well browned and crisp. Remove from the oven and let the duck rest for 5 minutes before carving. Carve the duck breasts crosswise into slices, and serve with the mango salsa.

meat & game

gremolata pork
with lemon spinach

4 boneless pork chops, 3 oz. each

1 tablespoon basil oil

2 oz. ciabatta bread, torn into pieces

¼ cup coarsely chopped flat-leaf parsley

grated zest of 1 unwaxed lemon

2 tablespoons olive oil

freshly ground black pepper

lemon spinach

8 oz. young spinach, washed, dried, and thinly sliced, about 2–3 cups

1 tablespoon extra virgin olive oil, plus extra for serving

freshly squeezed juice of ½ lemon

serves 4

In this recipe, which demonstrates one of the great advantages of sautéing, pork chops are coated in bread crumbs, and then sautéed gently to give a crisp outside while the meat remains tender inside.

Trim any excess fat from the pork chops, leaving a thin layer around the meat. Put each chop between 2 pieces of plastic wrap and, using a rolling pin, beat to ¼-inch thickness. Remove and discard the plastic wrap. Put the pork in a shallow dish, add the basil oil and black pepper. Turn to coat, cover, and refrigerate for 2 hours.

To make the bread crumbs, put the ciabatta pieces in a food processor and pulse to coarse crumbs. Put the bread crumbs, parsley, and lemon zest in a bowl, and mix. Add black pepper, to taste. Transfer to a plate and coat the pork with the crumb mixture, pressing gently until covered on both sides.

Heat the oil in a large skillet, add the pork, and cook for 2–3 minutes on each side or until the bread crumbs are golden and the pork is cooked through.

Put the spinach in a large bowl, add the olive oil and lemon juice, and toss to coat. Put a mound of spinach on each plate and top with the pork. Drizzle with the olive oil, season with pepper, and serve.

There are two ways to cook the pork. If you're in a hurry, use the fast-roast method, a favorite with many modern cooks. Alternatively, use the slow-cooking method, which keeps meat like pork moister and more tender. Instructions for both are given below.

italian pork tenderloin
with fennel and garlic

2 pork tenderloins, about 1 lb. each, trimmed

fennel and pepper seasoning

2 teaspoons fennel seeds

½ teaspoon coarse salt

5 black peppercorns

2 garlic cloves, crushed

⅓ cup extra virgin olive oil

serves 4

To make the seasoning, grind the fennel seeds, salt, and peppercorns with a mortar and pestle. Mash in the garlic and olive oil to form a paste. Make a few light slashes in each tenderloin and put onto a roasting tray. Rub the seasoning oil all over the pork and pour any remaining oil on top.

To fast-roast, cook on the middle shelf of a preheated oven at 425°F for 20 minutes, or until the internal temperature registers 150°F on an instant-read thermometer, or until there are no pink juices when you pierce the meat with a skewer. Baste the pork several times while roasting.

If following the slower method, cook in a preheated oven at 325°F for about 45 minutes or until done, as above. Baste several times.

For both methods, rest the pork for 10 minutes before slicing and serving.

3 tablespoons peanut or safflower oil

1½ lb. well trimmed boneless pork sparerib,
sliced into chunks

2 cups beef stock

hinleh (curry) paste

4–6 red bird's eye chiles, seeded and chopped,
or, if unavailable, use 1–2 cayenne chile peppers

5 garlic cloves, quartered

½ onion, coarsely chopped

2 inches fresh ginger root, peeled and grated

¼ teaspoon ground turmeric

2 inches fresh galangal, peeled and grated
(see recipe introduction)*

1 stalk of fresh lemongrass, outer leaves
discarded, the remainder very finely chopped

3 anchovies in oil, drained and finely chopped
plus a dash of fish sauce

to serve

a handful of Thai basil or cilantro

2 red bird's eye chiles, thinly sliced lengthwise,
or, if unavailable, use another tiny hot chile like
a cayenne chili pepper

boiled rice

serves 4

*Fresh galangal is available from Asian
stores and markets.

This curry is a Burmese specialty and doesn't include the coconut milk so typical of Southeast Asian cooking. It does use three root spices from the same family—turmeric, ginger, and galangal. In Burma and throughout Asia, all three are used fresh, but in the West, turmeric root is rarely available, so the ground form must be used. If you can't get fresh galangal, use additional fresh ginger.

burmese pork hinleh

To make the hinleh paste, put all the ingredients in a blender and grind to a paste, adding a dash of water to let the blades run. Alternatively, use a mortar and pestle.

Heat the oil in a large saucepan and add the paste. Stir-fry for several minutes. Add the pork and stir-fry to seal. Add the stock, bring to a boil, reduce the heat, and simmer gently, stirring occasionally, for 40–45 minutes, until cooked through but very tender.

Sprinkle with the herbs and chile and serve with boiled rice.

braised lamb shanks
with orange and marmalade

Meat cooked on the bone has a very different texture from the boned type where the meat can shrink back unimpeded into a tight ball. The meat remains stretched as it cooks and has a tender, far more open texture.

4 lamb shanks

4 tablespoons olive oil

3 garlic cloves, sliced

freshly squeezed juice of 2 oranges, about 1 cup

½ cup dry white wine

zest of 1 unwaxed lemon

3 tablespoons bitter orange marmalade

½ cup chicken stock or water

sea salt and freshly ground black pepper

a flameproof casserole dish

serves 4

Preheat a broiler until very hot. Brush the shanks with 3 tablespoons of the oil and season well, then broil, turning them as necessary until well-browned all over.

Heat the remaining oil in a flameproof casserole dish, add the garlic, and brown gently without burning. Add the shanks, orange juice, wine, and lemon zest. Bring to a boil on top of the stove, cover with a lid, then transfer to a preheated oven and cook at 350°F for 1 hour, or until the meat pulls away from the bone. Remove from the oven and place on the stovetop.

Using a slotted spoon, lift out the shanks and place on a plate and put them in a low oven to keep warm. Place the casserole dish over a burner and turn the heat to medium.

Add the marmalade to the casserole dish, stir until well blended, bring to a boil, and simmer until the liquid has been reduced to a coating glaze.

Return the shanks to the casserole dish and turn them in the glaze until well coated. Serve on warmed plates. Add the stock to the casserole dish, stir to scrape up the flavored bits left in the pan, then spoon it over the shanks. Serve with your choice of steamed vegetables and mashed sweet potatoes.

Depending on size, you may need two breasts per person—this is something you can decide when shopping. Cooking a whole pheasant is more economical and will serve two to three people, but involves all that last-minute carving and it never looks as good. If pheasant is hard to find, use guinea fowl.

roasted pheasant breasts
with bacon, shallots, and mushrooms

6 plump pheasant breasts

12 slices bacon

6 sprigs of thyme

3 fresh bay leaves, cut in half

2 tablespoons butter

1 tablespoon olive oil

12 small shallots

½ cup dry sherry

6 portobello mushrooms, quartered

6 thick slices French bread

8 oz. watercress, about 3–4 cups

sea salt and freshly cracked black pepper

serves 6

Remove the skin from the pheasant breasts and discard it. Wrap 2 slices of bacon around each breast, inserting a sprig of thyme and half a bay leaf between the pheasant and the bacon.

Put the butter and oil in a large flameproof roasting pan and set on top of the stove over high heat. Add the pheasant breasts, shallots, sherry, mushrooms, salt, and pepper. Turn the pheasant breasts in the mixture until they are well coated. Transfer to the upper rack of a preheated oven at 375°F and cook for 25 minutes.

Remove from the oven and let rest for 5 minutes.

Put the bread onto plates, then add the watercress, mushrooms, shallots, and pheasant. Spoon any cooking juices over them, and serve.

Broiling is the healthy way to cook sausages, with the fat draining away into the broiler tray. Turn them often, so that they cook through and brown evenly on the outside. You can make this with any good-quality sausages, but the gamey venison goes particularly well with the rich, red sauce.

venison sausages
with port and cranberry ragout

2 large leeks, cut into ¼-inch slices

2 tablespoons butter

1 tablespoon all-purpose flour

1 tablespoon sugar

1¼ cups red wine

3 tablespoons port

⅔ cup chicken or vegetable stock

a large sprig of rosemary

8 good-quality plump sausages, preferably venison

2 cups fresh or frozen cranberries

sea salt and freshly ground black pepper

Classic Creamy Mashed Potatoes (page 109), to serve

serves 4

Rinse the leeks well in a bowl of cold water, to remove any grit or dirt, then drain in a strainer. Melt the butter in a large saucepan. Add the leeks and gently sauté over medium heat, stirring frequently, for 8–10 minutes, until softened and slightly golden.

Preheat the broiler to a medium setting.

Add the flour to the pan of cooked leeks and cook, stirring, for 1 minute. Add the sugar, wine, port, stock, rosemary, and plenty of salt and black pepper. Bring to a boil, reduce the heat, and simmer for 15–20 minutes.

Meanwhile, cook the sausages under a preheated hot broiler, turning them frequently, for 15–20 minutes, until browned all over and cooked all the way through.

Add the cranberries to the pan and simmer for a further 5–6 minutes, until they begin to soften and pop. Add salt, pepper, and sugar to taste. Serve the sausages with the ragout and the mashed potatoes.

pan-grilled vietnamese beef
with sour cream and chile tomato relish

4 slices beef tenderloin steak, 1-inch thick, about 1 lb.

4 small orange-fleshed sweet potatoes, peeled and cut crosswise into 1-inch slices

marinade

2 tablespoons fish sauce

2 tablespoons mirin (Japanese sweet rice wine)

1 tablespoon toasted sesame oil

grated zest and juice of 1 unwaxed lime

chile tomato relish

4 ripe plum tomatoes, skinned and chopped

3 red bell peppers, peeled and chopped

6 red jalapeño chiles, seeded and chopped

3 inches fresh ginger root, peeled and grated

2 tablespoons salt

1 cup sugar

⅓ cup sherry vinegar

to serve

a few handfuls of salad greens

4 heaped tablespoons sour cream

serves 4

This combination of Vietnamese marinated beef, sour cream, steamed sweet potatoes, and spicy chile tomato relish is a terrific party piece.

To make the chile tomato relish, put all the ingredients in a food processor and pulse until coarsely chopped. Transfer to a saucepan, bring to a boil, skim off the foam, then reduce the heat and simmer for 30 minutes. Pour into hot sterilized jars (page 4), seal, and let cool. Use immediately or store in the refrigerator: it will keep for 2 weeks.

Mix the marinade ingredients in a shallow dish. Add the beef, cover, and set aside for at least 15 minutes. Turn over and marinate for at least another 15 minutes. Alternatively, marinate in the refrigerator overnight.

Heat a stove-top grill pan to medium-hot. Add the beef and cook for about 2 minutes on each side. The meat should be brown outside and rare in the middle. If you want it medium, cook for another 2 minutes.

Meanwhile, steam the sweet potatoes until a fork pierces them easily. Alternatively, boil in salted water, then drain.

To serve, put a handful of salad greens on each plate, add a steak and a scoop of sweet potatoes, then a spoonful of sour cream and 1–2 tablespoons chile tomato relish.

Steak always turns dinner into a special treat.
Make the blue cheese butter ahead of time,
then you can prepare the rest of the dish in
a matter of minutes.

steak with blue cheese butter

4 top loin or tenderloin steaks,
8 oz. each

sea salt and freshly ground
black pepper

oil, for sautéing (optional)

baby spinach salad, to serve

blue cheese butter

4 tablespoons unsalted butter,
softened

2 oz. soft blue cheese, such as
Gorgonzola, about ½ cup

¼ cup walnuts, finely ground
in a blender

2 tablespoons chopped fresh parsley

serves 4

To make the blue cheese butter, put the butter, cheese, walnuts, and parsley in a bowl and beat well. Season with salt and pepper to taste. Form into a log, wrap in foil, and chill for about 30 minutes.

Lightly season the steaks and cook on a preheated outdoor grill, or sauté in a little oil in a skillet on top of the stove, for 3 minutes on each side for rare, or 4–5 minutes for medium to well done.

Cut the butter into 8 slices. Put 2 slices of butter onto each cooked steak, wrap loosely with foil, and let rest for 5 minutes.

Serve the steaks with a salad of baby spinach.

Nothing beats a good homemade pie with tender pieces of meat in a delicious gravy. This one is topped with simple-to-make crisp suet crust and is a sure winner.

steak and mushroom pie

filling

3 tablespoons olive oil

2 onions, chopped

3 lb. stewing beef, cubed

8 oz. button mushrooms, about 2–2½ cups

1 tablespoon flour

½ teaspoon dried mixed herbs

1 teaspoon Worcestershire sauce

1 teaspoon English mustard, or Dijon

1¾ cups beef stock

sea salt and freshly ground black pepper

suet pastry dough

1⅔ cups self-rising flour

⅔ cup shredded suet or shortening

a 1-quart, deep pie dish

serves 4

To make the filling, heat the olive oil in a large skillet, add the onions, and sauté until softened but not browned. Transfer to a plate. Add a little more oil to the skillet if needed, then add the meat and sauté until browned and sealed. Add the mushrooms to the meat and sauté for about 5 minutes, then sprinkle in the flour and mix well to absorb all the oil.

Return the onions to the skillet and add the mixed herbs, Worcestershire sauce, mustard, salt, and pepper. Slowly pour in the stock, blending well. Bring to a boil, then lower the heat and simmer the mixture for 1½ hours.

When the meat is almost cooked, make the pastry dough. Sift the flour into a bowl, add the suet or shortening, salt, and pepper and mix well. Add about 5 tablespoons water and mix with a round-bladed knife until the mixture forms a dough. A little more water may be needed, but take care not to add too much since it will make the dough difficult to handle.

Transfer the cooked meat to the pie dish and set aside to cool.

Roll out the dough to a circle larger than the pie dish. Wet the lip of the dish, then cut thin strips of the dough from the trimmings, and press them onto the lip. Dampen the pastry lip, then lay the rolled dough over the pie and flute the edge with your fingers to seal. Trim, and make a small hole in the center. Bake in a preheated oven at 425°F for about 35 minutes, until golden brown.

Stews aren't difficult: Just put them on to cook and they look after themselves. This one makes a useful two-course meal. Serve some of the juices poured over pasta as an appetizer, then have the meat itself as an entrée. The stew improves if it is made the day before and reheated—real easy entertaining.

boeuf en daube

2 lb. beef, such as shoulder, cut into ½-inch thick slices

¼ cup extra virgin olive oil

4 garlic cloves, sliced

4 oz. thick bacon, cut into small dice, about ⅔ cup

3 carrots, cut in half lengthwise

12–16 baby onions, peeled

6 plum tomatoes, peeled, and thickly sliced

zest of 1 orange, removed in one piece

a bunch of fresh herbs, such as parsley, thyme, bay leaf, and rosemary, tied together with kitchen twine

½ cup walnut halves

1 cup robust red wine

2 tablespoons Cognac or brandy

¾ cup beef stock or water

6-inch square salt pork (optional)

chopped fresh parsley, to serve (optional)

a large flameproof casserole dish

serves 4–6

Cut the beef into pieces about the size of "half a postcard," as Elizabeth David advised—in other words 2½-inch squares. Heat the oil in a flameproof casserole dish and sauté the garlic, bacon, carrots, and onions for 4–5 minutes, or until aromatic and then remove from the casserole dish. Put a layer of meat into the casserole dish, then add half the sautéed vegetable mixture and a second layer of meat. Add the remaining vegetable mixture, the tomatoes, orange zest, bundle of herbs, and walnuts.

Put the wine in a small saucepan and bring to a boil. Add the Cognac or brandy and warm for a few seconds, shaking the pan a little, to let the alcohol cook away. Pour the hot liquids over the meat with just enough stock or water so that it's barely covered. Put the salt pork, if using, on top.

Heat the stew until simmering, then cover with foil and a lid and simmer gently for 2 hours or until the meat is fork tender and the juices rich and sticky.

The dish can also be cooked in the oven in a flameproof and ovenproof pot. Just bring to a boil over high heat, reduce to a simmer, cover with foil, replace the lid, and cook in a preheated oven at 300°F for 2½ hours, or until very tender.

Remove and discard the salt pork, which will have given a velvety quality to the sauce. Sprinkle with chopped parsley, if using. Serve hot on its own or with accompaniments such as pasta, Classic Creamy Mashed Potatoes (page 109), or boiled rice.

2 lb. boneless shoulder of lamb, trimmed of about half its fat and cut into 2-inch chunks

2⅔ cups chicken stock

2 tablespoons olive oil

1 large onion, coarsely chopped

4 garlic cloves, chopped

1 tablespoon ground cumin

1 tablespoon ground coriander

1 tablespoon hot paprika

16 oz. canned chopped tomatoes, 2 cups

1 cinnamon stick, broken in half

1 cup dried apricots

½ teaspoon freshly ground black pepper

3 large pieces of unwaxed orange zest

orange relish

2 oranges, separated into segments

1 red onion, chopped

1 red chile, finely chopped

leaves from a bunch of cilantro

1 tablespoon mint leaves, thinly chopped

to serve

½ cup pine nuts, lightly pan-toasted in a dry skillet

couscous

serves 4

A tagine is a North African stew cooked in a tall, conical pot of the same name. It is traditionally made over an open fire, but it also works well in the oven, or in a wok or sauté pan on top of the stove.

moroccan lamb tagine

Heat a large, nonstick sauté pan or wok until hot. Add half the lamb chunks and sear on all sides until brown. Using a slotted spoon, remove the browned lamb from the pan, put it on a plate, and set aside. Add about ½ cup of the chicken stock to the sauté pan or wok. Stir with a wooden spoon to remove all the flavorful sediment from the bottom, then pour out into a bowl and set aside. Add the remaining lamb to the pan and sear until brown, repeating the chicken stock process.

Return the pan to the heat and add the oil. When hot, add the onion and sauté gently for about 10 minutes until golden. Add the garlic and sauté for a further 2 minutes. Add the cumin, ground coriander, and paprika and sauté for a further 1 minute. Add the reserved browned lamb, tomatoes, cinnamon, apricots, pepper, orange zest, and remaining stock. Bring to a boil and cover with a lid. Reduce the heat and simmer very gently for about 2 hours until the meat is meltingly tender. Alternatively, if your pan and lid are ovenproof, cover with a lid and cook in a preheated oven at 300°F for about 2 hours, or until the meat is very tender.

Put all the relish ingredients in a bowl and mix. Serve the tagine sprinkled with pine nuts, accompanied by the relish and couscous.

pasta, rice, & noodles

Good olive oil and Mediterranean vegetables produce an easy, substantial pasta dish. No long simmering here: the tiny tomato halves are oven-roasted and the cubes of eggplant salted, then sautéed, to intensify the flavor. Handfuls of basil add the final flourish.

sicilian spaghetti

1 eggplant, about 12 oz., cut into ½-inch cubes

1 lb. cherry tomatoes, cut in half and seeded, about 2½–3 cups

½ cup extra virgin olive oil

⅓ cup crushed tomatoes (or juice)

2 garlic cloves, chopped

a large handful of basil leaves

14 oz. dried pasta, such as spaghetti or penne

sea salt and freshly ground black pepper

a baking tray

serves 4

Put the eggplant in a non-metallic bowl, then add 1 teaspoon salt and toss to combine. Set aside while you cook the tomatoes.

Pack the tomatoes, cut sides up, on a baking tray. Sprinkle with the remaining salt and 2 tablespoons of the oil, then roast in a preheated oven at 450°F for 10 minutes, or until wilted and aromatic.

Drain the eggplant and pat dry with paper towels. Put ¼ cup of the olive oil in a nonstick skillet and heat gently. Add the eggplant and cook, stirring, over high heat until frizzled and soft, about 8 minutes.

Add the roasted tomato halves, crushed tomatoes or juice, garlic, and black pepper. Cook, stirring, for 2–3 minutes, then tear up most of the basil leaves and stir through.

Meanwhile, bring a large saucepan of salted water to a boil, ready to add the pasta when the sautéed and roasted vegetables are half-cooked. Cook the pasta according to the instructions on the package.

Drain the cooked pasta, return it to the saucepan, and toss in the remaining olive oil. Divide between warmed bowls, spoon the sauce over it, add a few basil leaves, and serve.

pasta with melted ricotta and herby parmesan sauce

Pasta is the archetypal easy food. This one is fast and fresh, with the ricotta melting into the hot pasta and coating it like a creamy sauce. The pine nuts give it crunch, while the herbs lend it authentic flavor.

12 oz. dried penne or other pasta

¼ cup extra virgin olive oil

1 cup pine nuts, about 4 oz.

4 oz. arugula, thinly sliced, about 2½ cups

2 tablespoons chopped fresh parsley

2 tablespoons chopped fresh basil

8 oz. fresh ricotta cheese, about 1 cup, mashed

4 oz. freshly grated Parmesan cheese, about 2 cups

cracked black pepper

serves 4

Cook the pasta according to the instructions on the package.

Meanwhile, heat the olive oil in a skillet, add the pine nuts, and sauté gently until golden. Set aside.

Drain the cooked pasta, reserving ¼ cup of the cooking liquid, and return both to the pan. Add the pine nuts and their olive oil, the arugula, the herbs, the ricotta, half the Parmesan, and plenty of cracked black pepper. Stir until evenly coated.

Serve in warmed bowls, with the remaining cheese sprinkled on top.

herbed tagliatelle
with shrimp skewers

A lovely, summery dish, which makes the most of garden herbs. Serve the shrimp on skewers to make it an occasion (this also makes them easier to turn while cooking), although they can be cooked separately and added just before serving.

12 oz. dried pasta, such as tagliatelle, linguine, or fettuccine
20 raw jumbo shrimp, peeled, with tails on
2 garlic cloves, crushed
½ teaspoon red pepper flakes
¼ cup olive oil
1 lemon, cut into 4 wedges
1 teaspoon chopped fresh rosemary
2 tablespoons chopped flat-leaf parsley
1 tablespoon chopped fresh chives
a handful of torn arugula
sea salt and freshly ground black pepper

4 wooden skewers, soaked in water for 30 minutes

serves 4

Bring a large saucepan of water to a boil. Add a pinch of salt, then the pasta, and cook until al dente, or according to the timings on the package.

Meanwhile, put the shrimp in a bowl and add the garlic, red pepper flakes, 1 tablespoon of the oil, and salt and pepper to taste. Mix well, then thread 5 shrimp onto each skewer.

Preheat a stove-top grill pan until hot. Add the shrimp skewers to the hot pan and cook for 3 minutes on each side, until pink and cooked through. Remove and keep them warm in a low oven. Add the lemon wedges to the pan and cook quickly for 30 seconds on each side.

Drain the pasta and return it to the warm pan. Add the remaining oil, rosemary, parsley, chives, and arugula, along with salt and pepper to taste. Toss gently, then divide between 4 warmed bowls. Top each with a shrimp skewer and a lemon wedge for squeezing, then serve.

This is a one-pot-wonder, with a great combination of clean and fresh flavors. The spaghetti absorbs the rich stock, which means it tastes good as well as looking fantastic. Try this method using other boneless cuts.

guinea fowl and asparagus spaghetti

2 large tomatoes

10 oz. dried spaghetti

4 guinea fowl breasts, or chicken breasts, 4 oz. each

10 oz. asparagus, trimmed, about 10 spears

8 oz. fine green beans, about 1½–2 cups

¼ cup olive oil, plus extra to serve

3 oz. black olives, such as niçoise or kalamata, pitted and chopped, about ½ cup

sea salt and freshly ground black pepper

fresh shavings of Parmesan cheese, to serve

serves 4

Cut a cross in the top of each tomato, put in a bowl, and cover with boiling water. Drain after 30 seconds, then peel and chop.

Bring a large saucepan of water to a boil and add the spaghetti. Stir, then put the guinea fowl or chicken breasts on top of the spaghetti. Cover with a lid and simmer for 8 minutes, then add the asparagus and beans. Replace the lid and cook for a further 3 minutes, until the spaghetti, and guinea fowl or chicken, are cooked. Drain out the cooking liquid, reserving it for a soup or sauce, leaving everything else in the pan.

Lift out the guinea fowl or chicken and place on a carving board and cover loosely with foil. Place the pan, with the spaghetti and vegetables in it, over medium heat and add the oil, olives, tomatoes, salt, and pepper. Cook, stirring constantly, for 2 minutes, then transfer to warmed serving plates. Slice the guinea fowl or chicken, and arrange on top of the spaghetti. Top with Parmesan shavings, drizzle with olive oil, sprinkle with salt and pepper, then serve.

classic lasagne

1 lb. dried lasagne

10 oz. fresh mozzarella cheese, drained and diced, 2½–3 cups

¼ cup freshly grated Parmesan cheese

sea salt and freshly ground black pepper

bolognese sauce

½ oz. dried porcini mushrooms, rinsed

1 tablespoon olive oil

1 onion, finely chopped

1 lb. ground beef, 2 cups

2 oz. prosciutto, coarsely chopped, about ½ cup

⅓ cup Marsala wine or sherry

3 cups tomato sauce or tomato purée

béchamel sauce

1 quart milk

1 small garlic clove

4 tablespoons butter

⅓ cup all-purpose flour

a baking dish, about 12 x 8 x 3 inches

serves 8

Lasagne does take a while to prepare, but you can do everything ahead of time and then put it in the oven when you are ready.

To make the bolognese sauce, put the porcini in a bowl, cover with boiling water, and set aside for 20 minutes until softened. Heat the oil in a large saucepan, add the onion, and cook for 2 minutes. Add the ground beef and prosciutto and cook for 3–4 minutes, stirring until evenly browned. Drain the porcini, chop them, then add to the pan along with the Marsala or sherry, and tomato sauce or purée. Cover and simmer for 1 hour, stirring occasionally, until rich and dark. Add salt and pepper to taste.

Meanwhile, bring a large saucepan of lightly salted water to a boil and add the lasagne. Cook the pasta according to the instructions on the package. Drain, and set aside in a bowl of cold water until needed.

To make the béchamel sauce, put the milk and garlic into a small saucepan and heat gently until warm. Melt the butter in a separate saucepan, then stir in the flour and cook for 1 minute. Gradually add the warm milk, stirring constantly to make a smooth sauce. Bring to a boil, then simmer gently for 2–3 minutes. Remove and discard the garlic. Add salt and pepper to taste.

Put 3–4 tablespoons of the bolognese sauce in the baking dish, spread evenly across the bottom, and cover with a layer of cooked lasagne. Spoon some béchamel sauce over the lasagne, cover with a few pieces of mozzarella, and continue adding layers, starting with a layer of bolognese sauce and finishing with the béchamel sauce and mozzarella, until all the ingredients have been used. Sprinkle with pepper and Parmesan, then bake in a preheated oven at 375°F for 30 minutes or until the top is crusty and golden.

Couscous is extremely easy to cook. In this recipe, saffron is added to the boiling water, which not only adds a touch of luxury, but also gives the dish an attractive color.

couscous
with roasted chicken and vegetables

8 small chicken pieces, with excess fat removed

2 onions, cut into wedges

4 garlic cloves

1 eggplant, cut into chunks

2 zucchinis, sliced

1 cup frozen peas

leaves from a bunch of flat-leaf parsley, chopped

⅔ cup couscous

a pinch of saffron threads

olive oil, for roasting

sea salt and freshly ground black pepper

a heavy, flameproof roasting pan, lightly oiled

serves 4

Arrange the chicken pieces in the roasting pan. Cook in a preheated oven at 375°F for 10 minutes.

Lift out the chicken and set it on a plate. Put the onions, garlic, and eggplant in the pan and toss them in the cooking juices, drizzling with a little oil if necessary.

Return the chicken pieces to the pan and roast in the oven for a further 30 minutes, turning after 15 minutes to ensure even browning. Eight minutes before it's finished roasting, add the zucchinis, peas, and parsley and return it to the oven.

Pour 1¼ cups boiling water into a saucepan and put over high heat. Once it's boiling, add the couscous and saffron and simmer for 5 minutes. Drain thoroughly, transfer to a large serving dish, season with salt and pepper, and fluff up with a fork.

Arrange the cooked chicken and vegetables on top of the couscous, cover, and keep warm in a low oven.

Use a metal spoon to skim off any excess fat from the roasting pan. Put the pan over a burner and heat to simmering. Add ⅔ cup water, salt, and pepper, and boil for 4 minutes. Pour it over the chicken and couscous, and serve.

Pad Thai, probably the best-known of all Thai noodle dishes, takes only 5 minutes to cook. Use thick ribbon-like rice noodles ("rice sticks") for authenticity, or rice vermicelli or egg noodles. Tamarind, commonly used in Asian cooking, has a unique sour flavor, but you can substitute freshly squeezed lime juice.

pad thai noodles

¼ cup sunflower oil

4 eggs, lightly beaten

6 oz. dried thick rice noodles, soaked in warm water for 5 minutes, then drained

2 cups curly kale or collard greens or other leafy greens, tough central core removed, and leaves coarsely chopped

¼ cup tamarind paste or 2 tablespoons freshly squeezed lime juice

¼ cup sweet chile sauce

¼ cup light soy sauce

1 large carrot, grated, about 2 cups

4 oz. bean sprouts, trimmed and rinsed, about 2 cups

to serve

⅓ cup roasted peanuts, chopped

4 scallions, thinly sliced

cilantro leaves

serves 4

Heat a wok until very hot, then add the oil. Add the eggs and noodles and stir-fry for about 2 minutes, until the eggs are lightly scrambled. Add the remaining ingredients and stir-fry for a further 3–5 minutes, until the noodles are cooked.

Divide between 4 warmed bowls and serve sprinkled with the peanuts, scallions, and cilantro.

gingered chicken noodles

Most Asian noodle dishes take just a matter of minutes to cook—in fact, noodles made of rice flour or mung bean starch are ready almost instantly. Wheat-based noodles (such as egg noodles) take the most time, but even then, only about the same time as regular dried pasta.

2 tablespoons rice wine, such as Chinese Shaohsing or Japanese mirin

2 teaspoons cornstarch

12 oz. skinless chicken breasts

7 oz. Chinese dried egg noodles

3 tablespoons peanut or safflower oil

1 inch fresh ginger root, peeled and thinly sliced

4 oz. snow peas, thinly sliced

¼ cup chopped fresh garlic chives or chives

4 oz. cashews, about 1 cup, toasted in a dry skillet, then chopped

sauce

½ cup chicken stock

2 tablespoons dark soy sauce

1 tablespoon freshly squeezed lemon juice

1 tablespoon toasted sesame oil

2 teaspoons light brown sugar

serves 4

Put the rice wine and cornstarch in a bowl and mix well. Cut the chicken into small chunks, add to the bowl, stir well, and set aside to marinate while you prepare the remaining ingredients.

Prepare the noodles according to the instructions on the package, then drain and shake dry.

Put all the sauce ingredients in a small bowl and mix well.

Drain the chicken. Heat 1½ tablespoons of the oil in a wok or large skillet, then add the chicken and stir-fry for 2 minutes, or until golden. Scoop onto a plate and wipe the wok clean. Add the remaining 1½ tablespoons oil, ginger, and snow peas, and stir-fry for 1 minute. Return the chicken to the pan, then add the noodles and sauce. Heat through for 2 minutes. Add the garlic chives and cashews, stir well, and serve immediately.

Rice noodles cook very quickly, so be careful not to overcook them. Rinsing them in boiling water removes excess starch and keeps them in strands, not clumps.

warm thai crab rice noodles

8 oz. dried rice noodles, preferably thin ones

12 oz. canned crabmeat, drained, or 7 oz. fresh, about 1 cup

dressing

2 tablespoons canola or safflower oil

1 red serrano chile, seeded and finely chopped

1 green serrano chile, seeded and finely chopped

1-inch piece of fresh ginger root, peeled and finely chopped

grated zest of 1 unwaxed lime

freshly squeezed juice of 2 limes

1 tablespoon Thai fish sauce

leaves from a large bunch of cilantro

½ cup cashews, lightly toasted

sea salt and freshly ground black pepper

serves 4 as an appetizer or light entrée

Soak or cook the noodles as directed on the package. Meanwhile, start some water boiling, and put the crabmeat in a large bowl and set aside.

To make the dressing, put the oil in another bowl. Add the chiles, ginger, lime zest and juice, fish sauce, and cilantro. Stir, then add the dressing to the bowl of crabmeat. Add salt and black pepper to taste, and mix.

When the noodles are cooked, drain, and rinse them with the boiling water. Return the noodles to their bowl or saucepan, then add half the crab mixture and half the cashews. Toss well.

Divide the noodles between 4 plates or bowls, and top each with a spoonful of the remaining crab mixture. Sprinkle with the remaining nuts, and serve.

paella

2 tablespoons olive oil

1 onion, finely chopped

2 garlic cloves, crushed and chopped

4 oz. chorizo sausage, thickly sliced

4 skinless chicken pieces, trimmed

1 cup long-grain rice

a large pinch of saffron threads

2¾ cups chicken stock

1 cup white wine

12 mussels, cleaned

8 large shrimp

4 oz. squid, cleaned and cut into rings

2 lemons, the juice from 1, and the other cut into wedges

sea salt and freshly ground black pepper

a bunch of flat-leaf parsley, chopped, to serve

serves 4

This wonderful Spanish dish is very easy to make and a joy to eat. Don't be put off by the long list of ingredients—they are all readily available from your local supermarket. On special occasions, serve the paella with a gourmet salad mix, followed by fresh fruit and Spanish cheeses.

Heat the olive oil in a paella pan or large skillet. Add the onion, garlic, and chorizo. Cook over low heat until the onion is softened and translucent, about 5 minutes.

Add the chicken pieces and cook for about 5 minutes on each side until lightly browned.

Add the rice, saffron, and stock to the skillet and mix well. Bring the mixture to a boil, reduce the heat, and simmer for 15 minutes, stirring so the rice doesn't stick to the bottom of the skillet. Add some more stock if needed.

Add the white wine, mussels, shrimp, squid, salt, and pepper. Cover with a lid or piece of foil, and cook, without stirring, for a further 8–10 minutes. Stir the lemon juice into the paella. Top with the chopped parsley and serve from the pan with lemon wedges on the side.

desserts

Even if you never make desserts at any other time, you probably do when you have people to dinner. Perfect for a dinner party, these little plum fudge desserts can be prepared well ahead of time, then cooked just before serving.

plum fudge desserts

4 tablespoons unsalted butter

4–5 tablespoons honey

2 tablespoons heavy cream

2 tablespoons brown sugar

1 teaspoon apple pie spice, or a pinch of cinnamon plus a little freshly grated nutmeg

3 oz. fresh white bread crumbs, about 1½ cups

2 ripe plums, cut in half, pitted, and thinly sliced

sour cream or crème fraîche, to serve

4 ramekins (custard cups), to hold ⅔ cup each

a baking tray

serves 4

Put the butter, honey, and cream in a saucepan and heat until the butter is melted. Put the sugar, spice, and bread crumbs in a bowl and stir well.

Divide half of the butter-honey mixture between the ramekins, and top each with a layer of plum slices, and then half the bread crumb mix. Add the remaining plums and bread crumbs, then spoon the remaining butter-honey mixture on top.

Set on a baking tray and bake in a preheated oven at 400°F for 20 minutes. Remove from the oven and let cool for 5 minutes, then carefully unmold the desserts and serve with a spoonful of sour cream or crème fraîche.

1 cup mascarpone cheese

¼–½ cup confectioners' sugar,
or to taste

⅓ cup Vin Santo, plus extra
to serve

12 ripe figs

serves 6

This lovely, simple dish is best served when you can find very good-quality fresh figs, preferably straight from a tree. Vin Santo is an Italian sweet wine that marries well with the flavor of both the figs and the mascarpone. If you can't find it, you could also use port or cream sherry.

fresh figs
with vin santo and mascarpone

Put the mascarpone in a bowl, add the confectioners' sugar and Vin Santo, and beat until smooth. Set aside to infuse for 30 minutes, then transfer to a small serving bowl.

Cut the figs in half and arrange on a large serving platter with the bowl of mascarpone. Serve with the bottle of Vin Santo, for guests to help themselves.

This is a tart filled with an uncooked lemon curd and baked in the oven until just firm. For a party you could make really tiny ones instead of one large one. If you are making bite-size morsels, the crusts must be wonderfully thin so that they melt in the mouth.

1 recipe Sweet Rich Pie Dough (page 234)

1 egg, beaten, to seal the dough

sour cream or crème fraîche, to serve (optional)

lemon filling

6 extra large eggs

2⅓ cups sugar

finely grated zest and strained juice of 4 juicy unwaxed lemons

1¼ sticks unsalted butter, melted

a removable-bottomed fluted tart pan, 9 inches diameter

a baking tray

foil or parchment paper and baking beans

serves 8

classic lemon tart

Bring the dough to room temperature. Preheat the oven to 375°F.

Roll out the dough thinly on a lightly floured countertop, lift it off and line the tart pan with it. Chill or freeze the pan for 15 minutes. Line the pie shell with parchment paper, then fill with baking beans. Set on a baking tray and bake "blind" in the center of a preheated oven at 375°F for 10–12 minutes, then carefully remove the parchment paper and the baking beans. Bake for a further 5–7 minutes to dry out completely.

Brush with beaten egg, then bake again for 5–10 minutes, until set and shiny, to prevent the filling from making the crust soggy. Remove from the oven and lower the temperature to 300°F.

To make the lemon filling, put the eggs, sugar, lemon zest and juice, and butter into a food processor and blend until smooth.

Set the baked pie crust on a baking tray and pour in the filling. Bake in the oven for about 1 hour (it may need a little longer, depending on your oven), until just set. Remove from the oven and let cool completely before serving. Serve at room temperature, maybe with a spoonful of sour cream or crème fraîche, if using.

A tart named after the sisters who, as legend has it, created an upside-down apple tart by mistake! The type of apple used is crucial here—it must retain its shape during cooking and yet have a good flavor, such as Golden Delicious or Jonagolds.

tarte des demoiselles tatin

1 lb. frozen puff pastry sheets, thawed

1¼ cups sugar

1½ sticks chilled unsalted butter, thinly sliced, about ⅔ cup

5–5½ lb. evenly-sized dessert apples, peeled, cut in half, and cored

crème fraîche, to serve

nonstick parchment paper

a baking tray

a cast-iron skillet or tarte tatin dish, 11 inches diameter

serves 6

Roll out the dough on nonstick parchment paper to a circle about 12 inches in diameter, slide onto a baking tray, and chill. Sprinkle the sugar over the bottom of the skillet or tarte tatin dish. Cover with the sliced butter.

Add the apple halves to the outside edge of the pan: set the first one at an angle, almost on its edge, then arrange the others all around the edge so that they slightly overlap and butt up against each other. Add another ring of apples inside, so that the pan is almost filled, then fill the gap in the center. The apples should cover the surface of the pan. They look awkward and bulky, but will cook down and meld together later.

Put the pan over gentle heat and cook for about 45 minutes, until the sugar and butter have caramelized and the apples have softened underneath. (Check every now and then and adjust the heat if necessary. The juices will gradually bubble up the sides; keep cooking until they are a dark amber.)

Remove the dough from the fridge and lay it over the apples in the pan. Tuck the edges down into the pan, making the rim of the tart. Prick the top of the dough here and there with a fork, then set the pan on the baking tray. Bake in a preheated oven at 375°F for 25–30 minutes, until the crust is risen and golden.

Remove the pan from the oven and immediately invert onto a warm serving plate. Replace any apple slices that stick to the pan. Serve warm, not hot, with crème fraîche.

sticky chocolate pecan pie

1½ cups all-purpose flour, plus extra for dusting

a pinch of salt

1 tablespoon sugar

1 stick unsalted butter, chilled and cut into small pieces, ½ cup

1 extra large egg yolk, mixed with 1 tablespoon cold water

vanilla ice cream or whipped cream, to serve

chocolate filling

3 tablespoons unsalted butter, softened

¾ cup firmly packed light brown sugar

⅔ cup corn syrup

3 extra large eggs, beaten

1 teaspoon vanilla extract

4 squares semisweet chocolate, melted

1 cup pecans

a removable-bottomed tart pan, 9 inches diameter, well buttered

parchment paper and baking beans or dried beans

serves 8

Incredibly rich and gooey, this is a real treat. The short, crumbly dough is simple to make in a food processor, and the filling has a wonderfully fudgy taste and texture. Use a freshly opened package of pecans for best results.

To make the dough in a food processor, put the flour, salt, sugar, and butter in the bowl and blend until the mixture looks like fine crumbs. With the machine running, add the egg yolk and water through the feed tube. Run the machine until the dough comes together. If there are dry crumbs, add a teaspoon or so extra water.

Put the dough onto a floured countertop and, using a rolling pin, roll out to a large circle about 2 inches larger than the tart pan, then use to line the pan. Prick the bottom of the pie crust with a fork, then chill for 15 minutes.

Line the pie crust with a sheet of nonstick parchment paper, then fill with baking beans or dried beans. Bake "blind" in a preheated oven at 350°F for about 12 minutes, then carefully remove the paper and beans. Bake for a further 10 minutes, until lightly golden and just firm. Remove from the oven and let cool while making the filling.

Put the butter, sugar, and corn syrup in a mixing bowl and, using a wooden spoon or electric mixer, beat until smooth. Gradually beat in the eggs and then the vanilla extract. Stir in the melted chocolate, followed by the pecans.

Pour the mixture into the prepared pie crust and bake in a preheated oven at 350°F for 35 minutes, until just firm to the touch. Remove from the oven and let cool—the filling will sink slightly. Serve warm or at room temperature, with some vanilla ice cream or whipped cream.

A delicious finale for a lovely summertime dinner, serve this very light cake with piles of berries and whipped cream.

italian chocolate amaretto torta

4 squares bittersweet chocolate, chopped

2 tablespoons Amaretto liqueur (optional)

1 stick unsalted butter, at room temperature, ½ cup

½ cup plus 1 tablespoon sugar

3 extra large eggs, separated

2 oz. (about 10) amaretti cookies, crushed

½ cup all-purpose flour, sifted, plus extra for flouring

to serve

whipped cream

blueberries or raspberries

a removable-bottomed cake pan, 8 inches diameter, buttered, bottom lined with parchment paper, then floured

serves 8

Put the chocolate and Amaretto in a heatproof bowl, and set it over a pan of steaming but not boiling water, and let it melt (do not let the bottom of the bowl touch the water). Alternatively, use a double boiler. Remove the bowl from the heat, stir gently, and let cool.

Put the butter and the ½ cup sugar in a mixing bowl and, using a wooden spoon or electric mixer, beat until very light and fluffy. Beat in the egg yolks one at a time, then stir in the cooled chocolate. When thoroughly blended, use a large metal spoon to fold in the crushed cookies and flour.

Put the egg whites into a spotlessly clean, grease-free bowl and beat with an electric beater until stiff peaks form. Beat in the remaining 1 tablespoon sugar to make a stiff, glossy meringue, then fold into the cake mixture in 3 batches.

Transfer the mixture to the prepared pan and bake in a preheated oven at 350°F for 30–35 minutes, until just firm to the touch. Let cool in the pan for 10 minutes, then remove from the pan and transfer to a wire rack to cool completely.

Sprinkle with confectioners' sugar and serve slightly warm or at room temperature, with whipped cream and fresh berries. Best eaten within 3 days. Not suitable for freezing.

You can make the crêpes for this heartwarming dessert ahead of time—keep them in the refrigerator for up to two days, separated by squares of wax paper. Alternatively, freeze the crêpes after they have cooled, and remove from the freezer thirty minutes before using.

hot whiskey crêpes
with raspberries

½ cup all-purpose flour

a pinch of salt

1 large egg

⅔ cup milk

2 teaspoons peanut oil

1¼ cups freshly squeezed orange juice

2 tablespoons honey

1 tablespoon butter

3 tablespoons whiskey

1¼ cups fresh raspberries

confectioners' sugar, for dusting

cream or plain yogurt, to serve

serves 4

Sift the flour and salt into a large bowl. Make a well in the center and crack the egg into the well. Gradually beat in the milk to form a smooth batter.

Heat a medium, nonstick skillet. Add a little oil and wipe out with a paper towel. Pour enough batter into the pan to coat the bottom, then cook for about 1 minute. Loosen the edges with a spatula, flip the crêpe, and cook for 1 minute more. Transfer to a plate and repeat with the remaining mixture to make 3 more crêpes. Set aside.

Pour the orange juice into the skillet and add the honey and butter. Bring to a boil, reduce the heat, and simmer for 5 minutes to concentrate the flavors and thicken the sauce slightly. Stir in the whiskey.

Carefully fold each crêpe in half, then in half again to make a triangle, and slide them into the simmering sauce. Heat for 30 seconds to warm through.

Transfer the crêpes and sauce to a serving plate and sprinkle with raspberries. Dust lightly with confectioners' sugar and serve with cream or plain yogurt.

Strawberries Romanov is a classic French dish. This sundae version is elegant enough to grace any dinner party.

romanov parfait

8 oz. strawberries, about 2 cups

2 tablespoons orange-flavor liqueur, such as Cointreau, Grand Marnier, or Triple Sec

1½ tablespoons confectioner's sugar

½ cup heavy cream

a few drops of vanilla extract

4–8 scoops strawberry or vanilla ice cream

serves 4

Rinse the strawberries, pat dry with paper towels, and reserve 4 of the berries for decoration. Hull the remaining berries and cut them in half (always rinse before hulling, not after, or the strawberries will fill with water).

Put the cut berries in a bowl and sprinkle with the liqueur and 1 tablespoon of the confectioner's sugar. Set aside for 30 minutes.

Whip the cream with the vanilla and the remaining confectioner's sugar until firm peaks form. Cover and chill until ready to use.

To serve, spoon the berries into small glass dishes, top with ice cream, whipped cream, and a reserved strawberry, cut in half.

This subtle ice cream has only four ingredients—five if you count the lime zest—yet tastes heavenly. It is perfect for serving after any Asian-style entrée, such as Green Thai Vegetable Curry (page 94).

coconut ice cream

2 cups milk

1 cup sugar

2 cups unsweetened, canned coconut milk

1 tablespoon dark rum or fresh lime juice

thin strips of unwaxed lime zest or lime wedges, to serve

ice cream maker (optional)

serves 8

Put half the milk and all the sugar into a saucepan and bring to a boil, stirring until the sugar is dissolved. Remove from the heat. Stir in the remaining milk and the coconut milk. Place the saucepan in a bowl of ice water to cool. Stir in the rum or fresh lime juice.

Pour the mixture into an ice cream maker. Churn for 25–40 minutes, or according to the manufacturer's instructions, until firm and silky. Alternatively, freeze in plastic trays until the mixture is hard at the edges, but soft in the center. Remove, scoop it into a bowl and stir well, then scoop back into the trays and refreeze as before. Repeat and refreeze.

Serve in bowls, glasses, or cones, topped with strips of lime zest, or with lime wedges for squeezing.

party food
& drink

You can really taste the difference in homemade hummus, especially this deluxe, caper-topped version.

luxury hummus

Put the chickpeas, tahini paste, and garlic in a food processor and blend until smooth. Add the lemon juice along with 3 tablespoons of the oil, and 1 tablespoon boiling water. Blend until very smooth. Add plenty of salt and black pepper. Put the parsley, capers, red pepper flakes, and the remaining olive oil into a bowl and mix well.

Put a mound of the hummus on each grilled pita bread and top with a spoonful of the parsley-caper mixture. Drizzle with olive oil and serve with lemon wedges.

15 oz. canned chickpeas, rinsed and drained, about 2 cups

3 tablespoons tahini paste

2 garlic cloves, coarsely chopped

freshly squeezed juice of 1 lemon

4 tablespoons extra virgin olive oil, plus extra to drizzle

a large bunch of flat-leaf parsley, coarsely chopped

2 tablespoons capers, rinsed and drained

½ teaspoon crushed hot red pepper flakes

sea salt and freshly ground black pepper

to serve

pita bread, grilled

1 lemon, cut into wedges

serves 4 as an appetizer

If you have fennel flowering in your garden, use the whole seed heads for this dish. Otherwise, use fennel seeds.

green olives with fennel

Pack most of the olives loosely into the jar(s) using tongs or a spoon.

Put the oil in a heavy saucepan and heat to 350°F or until a small cube of bread turns golden brown in about 40 seconds.

Using a slotted spoon, lower the cut garlic heads and the fennel flower heads into the oil. Let them sizzle briefly, for about 30 seconds, then lift them out and divide evenly between the jar(s). Scatter in the peppercorns, fennel seeds, and cloves. Top up with the remaining olives.

Pour the sizzling hot oil carefully over the olives until covered. Let cool for about 2 minutes, then pour the remaining oil carefully into the jar(s) until completely filled. Let cool, uncovered, and undisturbed. Seal tightly and store in a cool, dark cupboard until ready to serve.

3 cups imported preserved green olives, washed and dried with paper towels, then pricked with a fork, 18 oz.

2 cups extra virgin olive oil

2 whole heads of fresh garlic, cut in half crosswise

4–8 fresh fennel flower heads, seeds intact (optional)

3 tablespoons black peppercorns, cracked or coarsely crushed

2 tablespoons fennel seeds

1 teaspoon cloves

1 quart jar or 2 pint jars, sterilized (page 4)

makes 1 large or 2 small jars

potato skins with green dip

The cheese can be either melted and soft, or crisp and crunchy—keep checking and remove at the right moment. Save the potato middles for making mashed potatoes.

12 large baking potatoes

¾ cup olive oil

14 oz. sharp Cheddar cheese, grated, 3½–4 cups

green dip

1¾ cups sour cream

2 bunches of chives, chopped

2 bunches of scallions, chopped

a bunch of flat-leaf parsley, chopped

sea salt and freshly ground black pepper

a baking tray, lightly oiled

serves 24

Using a small, sharp knife, pierce each potato right through the middle. Bake in a preheated oven at 350°F for 1 hour 10 minutes, or until completely cooked. Remove and set aside until cool enough to handle. Cut each potato in half lengthwise and, using a spoon, scoop out the soft potato middles, leaving a thin layer lining the skin. Cut each skin half into 4 wedges, then cover and chill until needed.

Brush oil over the potato skins and arrange in a single layer on the prepared baking tray. Bake at the top of a preheated oven at 425°F for 30 minutes until golden, moving the potatoes around occasionally so they cook evenly. Remove from the oven and reduce the heat to 400°F. Sprinkle with cheese and return to the oven for 5–10 minutes, until the cheese is melted or crunchy, checking after 5 minutes if you want it melted.

To make the dip, put the sour cream, chives, scallions, and parsley in a bowl. Add salt and pepper to taste and mix well. Serve with the potato skins for dipping.

slow-roasted tomato and herb tartlets with feta

1 recipe Pâte Brisée Dough (page 235)

slow-roasted tomatoes

12–15 large ripe cherry tomatoes

2 garlic cloves, finely chopped

1 tablespoon dried oregano

¼ cup olive oil

sea salt and freshly ground black pepper

herby cheese filling

3 oz. full-fat soft cheese with garlic and herbs, such as Boursin, ⅓ cup

1 large egg, beaten

⅔ cup heavy cream

¼ cup chopped fresh mixed herbs, such as parsley, basil, or chives

3 oz. feta cheese, about ¾ cup

sea salt and freshly ground black pepper

tiny sprigs of thyme or cut chives, to serve

a plain cookie cutter, 2 inches diameter

2 mini-muffin pans, 12 cups each

a baking tray

makes 24 tartlets

Tiny tartlets are great to serve with cocktails. These look stunning and have a secret pocket of feta cheese lurking in the creamy, herby filling underneath the tomatoes. Make double quantity of the roasted tomatoes—they keep well in the refrigerator and are great in salads.

Bring the dough to room temperature. Roll out the dough as thinly as possible on a lightly floured countertop. Use the cookie cutter to stamp out 24 circles. Line the muffin cups with the dough circles, then prick the bottoms, and chill or freeze for 15 minutes. Bake blind following the method on page 203, then remove from the pans and let cool. (The shells will keep for up to 1 week in an airtight tin, but reheat to crisp before filling.)

Turn the oven down to 325°F. Cut the tomatoes in half horizontally. Arrange, cut side up, on a baking tray. Put the chopped garlic, oregano, olive oil, and lots of pepper in a bowl and mix well, then spoon or brush over the cut tomatoes. Bake slowly in the oven for 1½–2 hours, checking every now and then. They should be slightly shrunk and still a brilliant red color—if too dark, they will taste bitter. (Use the tomatoes right away or pack in a storage jar and cover with olive oil.)

Put the soft cheese in a bowl, add the egg, cream, and chopped herbs, and beat until smooth. Season well. Cut the feta into 24 small cubes that will fit inside the tartlet shells. When ready to bake, set the tartlets on a baking tray, put a cube of feta into each one, and top with the garlic and herb mixture. Bake in the preheated oven for 15–20 minutes or until the filling is set. Top each with a tomato half, a sprinkle of the cooking juices, and a thyme sprig or chive stem. Serve warm.

miniature spring rolls

Spring rolls should be lean, crisp, and refreshing, and make effortless party snacks. Serve them with your favorite dipping sauces, such as chile sauce, soy sauce, or fish sauce.

2 cups fresh bean sprouts

½ cup scallions, finely sliced

¾ cup carrots, finely sliced

¾ cup bamboo shoots, fresh or soaked, finely sliced

1 cup fresh shiitake mushrooms, stems discarded, caps thinly sliced

2 inches fresh ginger root, thinly sliced

3 tablespoons peanut oil, plus extra for frying

2 oz. firm tofu, thinly diced, about ½ cup

2 teaspoons sugar

1 tablespoon light soy sauce

1 tablespoon Chinese rice wine or dry sherry

20 spring roll wrappers or wonton wrappers

2 tablespoons flour

2 tablespoons water

makes 36–40

Blanch the bean sprouts for 1 minute in boiling water, then refresh in ice water. Top and tail them, discarding the ends. Put in a bowl, add the other vegetables and the ginger, and mix gently.

Heat the 3 tablespoons oil, add the vegetables, and stir-fry for 1–1½ minutes. Add the tofu, sugar, soy sauce, and rice wine, and cook for 1 minute longer. Cool. Divide into 8 portions (each will be enough for 5 spring rolls).

Cut each wrapper in half diagonally to form triangles. Put 1 piece of filling on the long side, a third of the way from the edge. Fold the long side over the filling, then fold over the side flaps. Roll up. Mix the flour and water and dab a little of the mixture on the loose end of the roll. Press to seal. Set the spring rolls on a lightly floured surface, not touching, until all are made.

Heat the oil to 375°F or a little hotter, but do not let it smoke. Deep-fry the rolls, 8–10 at a time, for about 3–4 minutes. Remove using a wire strainer, drain on crumpled paper towels, and keep warm in a low oven. Let the oil reheat before cooking the next batch.

When all the spring rolls have been cooked, serve with your choice of dips.

baby pizzas

4 cups all-purpose flour

2 packages fast-action or rapi-rise dry yeast, 1½ tablespoons

1 teaspoon sea salt

¼ cup extra virgin olive oil

toppings

1 cup fresh tomato sauce, tapenade, or sun-dried tomato pesto

1 cup sautéed spinach, arugula, or roasted peppers

½ cup black olives and/or capers

¼ cup canned anchovies, cut in half lengthwise, and/or toasted pine nuts

8 garlic cloves, chopped

1–2 tablespoons chopped fresh rosemary, sage, or thyme

1 cup mozzarella cheese, drained and cubed

1 cup extra virgin olive oil

sea salt and freshly ground black pepper

2 baking trays, lightly oiled
a round cookie cutter, 2–3 inches diameter

makes 32–40

There's nothing better than homemade pizzas. These are incredibly easy to make—all you need is a food processor. You can prepare large ones, but small ones like these make great party food and everyone can taste a different topping.

To make the dough, put the flour, yeast, and salt in a food processor. Pulse briefly to sift the dry ingredients. Add the olive oil and 1½ cups lukewarm water. Blend in short bursts for 15 seconds to form a soft mass, not a ball.

Turn out onto a floured countertop, then knead by hand for 2 minutes, slamming down the dough 2-3 times to help develop the gluten. Put the dough in a clean, oiled bowl. Turn it over once to coat with oil. Put the bowl of dough into a large plastic bag, seal, and let rise in a warm, draftfree spot until doubled in size, about 1½ hours.

Put the dough on the countertop and punch it down with oiled hands. Divide into half. Pat and roll out each piece to a circle about ⅛ inch thick. Push dimples all over it with your fingers.

Using the cookie cutter, cut out about 16 small disks. Set them on a baking tray. Top each one with ½–1 teaspoon sauce, tapenade, or pesto. Add spinach, arugula, or roasted peppers, then a choice of olives, capers, anchovies, or pine nuts. Add garlic, herbs, or cheese. Season to taste, and sprinkle with olive oil. Repeat, using the second half of the dough on a second baking tray.

Set aside for 15-20 minutes, then bake at 475°F for 12-15 minutes or until the bottoms are blistered and crisp, the toppings aromatic, and the cheese melted. Serve hot.

pimm's

1 part Pimm's

3 parts ginger ale, lemonade,
or club soda

borage flowers

curls of cucumber peel

sliced lemons

sprigs of mint

serves from 1 to a party

This traditional English summertime drink is perfect for parties. When borage is in flower, freeze the pretty blue blossoms in ice cubes for out-of-season Pimm's drinks. Allow 1 cup per drink, and at least 2 drinks per person—but be prepared for repeat orders!

Put all the ingredients in a pitcher of ice, stir, and serve.

champagne cocktails

The ultimate party drink, champagne is always a
great hit and these cocktails are delicious. You
could use another sparkling wine, if you preferred.

1 teaspoon of a liqueur such as
Poire William, peach or strawberry
liqueur, framboise, Midori, blue
curaçao, or Galliano, and the pulp
of 1 passionfruit

alternatively, ¼ cup fruit juice,
such as pear, pineapple, peach,
or apricot

champagne

serves 1

Put the liqueur or fruit juice in a
champagne flute or coupé, and top
up with champagne.

sea breeze

This is a modern, thirst-quenching variation on the classic Screwdriver. Any combination of vodka and freshly squeezed juices will work in creating a Breeze to suit your personal taste.

2 oz. vodka
cranberry juice
fresh grapefruit juice
1 lime wedge

serves 1

Pour a large shot of vodka in a highball glass filled with ice. Three-quarters fill the glass with cranberry juice, and top with fresh grapefruit juice. Garnish with a lime quarter and serve with a straw.

mint mojito

Zesty and refreshing, a Mojito is the perfect summer drink to refresh and revive. Before serving, strain through a fine-mesh strainer to remove all the chopped mint (it's the mint juice that gives it such an amazing color).

Put the rum, lime juice, sugar or sugar syrup, mint leaves, and ice cubes in a blender, zap well, then strain into a glass half-filled with ice.

Serve straight or topped up with sparkling spring water, with a sprig of mint and a curl of lime zest.

¼ cup white rum

freshly squeezed juice of 1 lime

1 tablespoon sugar or sugar syrup

leaves from a large bunch of mint

ice cubes

sparkling spring water (optional)

mint sprigs and lime zest, to serve

serves 1

The usual way of serving margaritas is to rim the glasses with salt. This is optional, but a twist of lime is absolutely crucial! Some people like to add a dash of sugar, though this may depend on the flavor of the limes.

margarita

1 part tequila

1 part triple sec or other orange liqueur, such as Cointreau

2 parts freshly squeezed lime juice, thinned with water, if you like

crushed ice or ice cubes

a twist of lime, to serve

serves 1

Shake or blend the tequila, triple sec, lime juice, and crushed ice or ice cubes. Pour into a salt-rimmed glass, if you like, and serve with a twist of lime.

Variations:

Frozen Margarita

In a blender, whizz 1 part tequila, 1 part Grand Marnier, 2 parts freshly squeezed lime juice, 2 parts ice, and sugar to taste, then pour into ice-frosted, salt-rimmed glasses.

Cranberry Margarita

In a blender, whizz 1 part each of tequila, Cointreau, and freshly squeezed lime juice along with 2 parts of cranberry juice, plus ice and sugar to taste. Serve immediately in a salt-rimmed glass, if you like.

pastry dough basics
sweet rich pie dough

This makes a wonderfully light and crumbly crust. It is best used for richer pies and tarts, or where it is more than just a carrier for the filling, and the taste of the crust is important.

2 cups all-purpose flour,
plus extra for dusting

½ teaspoon salt

2 tablespoons confectioners' sugar

9 tablespoons unsalted butter,
chilled and diced

2 large egg yolks

2 tablespoons ice water

*makes about 14 oz. pastry dough,
enough for two 8-inch pie crusts*

Put the flour, salt, and sugar in a food processor, add the butter, and blend until the mixture looks like fine bread crumbs. Mix the egg yolks with the ice water and add to the machine. Blend again until it begins to form a ball—add another tablespoon of water if it is too dry, and blend again.

Tip the mixture onto a lightly floured countertop. Knead lightly with your hands until smooth, then shape into a flattened ball. Wrap in plastic wrap and chill for 30 minutes before rolling.

2 cups all-purpose flour

1 teaspoon salt

9 tablespoons unsalted butter, softened

1 extra-large egg yolk

2½–3 tablespoons ice water

makes about 14 oz. pastry dough,

enough for two 8-inch pie crusts

pâte brisée dough

This dough has a fine texture and should be rolled out thinly—to about ⅛ inch. Don't be tempted to leave out the water in this recipe—it makes the dough stronger and easier to handle in the end.

Sift the flour and salt together onto a sheet of wax paper.

Put the butter and egg yolk in a food processor and blend until smooth. Add the water and blend again. Add the flour and salt, and pulse until just mixed.

Tip the mixture onto a lightly floured countertop and knead gently until smooth. Form into a ball, flatten slightly, and wrap in plastic wrap.

Chill in the refrigerator for at least 30 minutes. Let the dough return to room temperature before rolling out.

index

conversion charts

Weights and measures have been rounded up or
down slightly to make measuring easier.

Volume equivalents:

American	Metric	Imperial
1 teaspoon	5 ml	
1 tablespoon	15 ml	
¼ cup	60 ml	2 fl.oz.
⅓ cup	75 ml	2½ fl.oz.
½ cup	125 ml	4 fl.oz.
⅔ cup	150 ml	5 fl.oz. (¼ pint)
¾ cup	175 ml	6 fl.oz.
1 cup	250 ml	8 fl.oz.

Weight equivalents:

Imperial	Metric
1 oz.	25 g
2 oz.	50 g
3 oz.	75 g
4 oz.	125 g
5 oz.	150 g
6 oz.	175 g
7 oz.	200 g
8 oz. (½ lb.)	250 g
9 oz.	275 g
10 oz.	300 g
11 oz.	325 g
12 oz.	375 g
13 oz.	400 g
14 oz.	425 g
15 oz.	475 g
16 oz. (1 lb.)	500 g
2 lb.	1 kg

Measurements:

Inches	Cm
¼ inch	5 mm
½ inch	1 cm
¾ inch	1.5 cm
1 inch	2.5 cm
2 inches	5 cm
3 inches	7 cm
4 inches	10 cm
5 inches	12 cm
6 inches	15 cm
7 inches	18 cm
8 inches	20 cm
9 inches	23 cm
10 inches	25 cm
11 inches	28 cm
12 inches	30 cm

Oven temperatures:

110°C	(225°F)	Gas ¼
120°C	(250°F)	Gas ½
140°C	(275°F)	Gas 1
150°C	(300°F)	Gas 2
160°C	(325°F)	Gas 3
180°C	(350°F)	Gas 4
190°C	(375°F)	Gas 5
200°C	(400°F)	Gas 6
220°C	(425°F)	Gas 7
230°C	(450°F)	Gas 8
240°C	(475°F)	Gas 9

credits

Photographs

a=above, b=below, r=right, l=left, c=center

Peter Cassidy Pages 3l, 3r, 9al, 16, 20, 25al, bl, bc, & br, 27, 32–33, 35, 36, 39, 43ac, ar, & bl, 47, 53, 54, 57cl, 58, 61, 69, 76, 77, 78, 80, 81al, ac, ar, & c, 95, 103, 108, 111ar, cr, br, bc, & bl, 113, 114, 116, 119, 123, 127, 129, 132, 133al, ac, & ar, 135, 136, 140, 144, 148, 150, 151al, ac, br, bl, & cl, 153, 154, 157, 162, 165, 170, 172, 175cl & bl, 176, 179, 190, 193, 197al, ar, br, bl, & cl, 198, 210, 217br, 218, 219, 227

Debi Treloar Pages 1, 2, 3cl, 6, 7, 8, 9ac, c, & br, 25ar, 56, 57bl, bc, & br, 70, 73, 74, 111al, 120, 133bl, 143, 151ar, 161, 169, 175ar & bc, 183, 186, 194, 213, 216, 217 all above & bl, 220

William Lingwood Pages 21, 31, 40–41, 43cr, 83, 86, 87, 98, 102, 112, 117, 130, 138–139, 149, 158–159, 174, 175al & br, 180, 184–185, 203, 228, 229, 230, 231, 234, 236–239

Philip Webb Pages 11, 28–29, 44–45, 48–49, 50, 65, 66, 81br, 91, 92, 99, 100, 104–105, 107, 189

Ian Wallace Pages 9ar, 12, 14, 15, 19, 22, 57ar, 124, 133br, 147, 166, 201, 240

Martin Brigdale Pages 81bl, 96, 202, 205, 206, 209, 223, 235

David Brittain Pages 3 background, 25c, 57al, 217cl

Jean Cazals Pages 62, 81bc, 82, 88

Craig Robertson Pages 52, 85, 97, 200

Jeremy Hopley Pages 42, 214, 224

David Montgomery Pages 141, 196, 197ac

Gus Filgate Page 24, 30

David Loftus Pages 5, 133cl

Caroline Arber Page 26

Henry Bourne Page 4

Dan Duchars Page 9bl

Tom Leighton Page 43br

James Merrell Page 233

Pia Tryde Page 110

Simon Walton Page 43al

Francesca Yorke Page 3cr

Recipes

CELIA BROOKS BROWN
Pancakes
Lemon potato latkes with gingered avocado crème
Celeriac, saffron, and orange soup
Shiitake and field mushroom soup with madeira and thyme
Mexican gazpacho
Caesar salad
Warm chickpea salad
Pumpkin and tofu laksa
Roasted teriyaki tofu steaks
Minted char-grilled zucchini
Chile greens with garlic crisps
Provençal roasted vegetables
Lemon-roasted baby potatoes
Pad Thai noodles

MAXINE CLARK
Smoked salmon and lemon pepper cream crostini
Roquefort tart with walnut and toasted garlic dressing
Classic lemon tart
Tarte Tatin
Slow-roasted tomato and herb tartlets with feta
Sweet rich pie dough
Pâte brisée dough

LINDA COLLISTER
Italian chocolate amaretto torta
Sticky chocolate pecan pie

CLARE FERGUSON
Shrimp with parsley and lemon
Bresaola and arugula with olive oil and Parmesan
Spicy Thai chicken soup
Fresh green salad
Warm chicken and chorizo salad
Catalan spinach
Stir-fried chicken with greens
Boeuf en daube
Sicilian spaghetti
Coconut ice cream
Green olives with fennel
Miniature spring rolls
Baby pizzas

SILVANA FRANCO
Herbed tagliatelle with shrimp skewers
Classic lasagne

MANISHA GAMBHIR HARKINS
Butternut squash soup with allspice and pine nuts
Andalusian chickpea soup with chorizo, paprika, and saffron
Mozzarella, tomato, and basil salad
Baked eggplant and tomato stacks
Chickpea and tomato masala with beans and coriander
Italian pork tenderloin with fennel and garlic
Burmese pork hinleh

ELSA PETERSEN-SCHEPELERN
Grilled polenta with grilled peppers
Pan-grilled Vietnamese beef with sweet potatoes, crème fraîche and chile tomato relish
Romanov parfait
Pimm's
Champagne cocktail
Mint mojito
Margarita

LOUISE PICKFORD
Waffles with maple syrup ice cream
Pecan and chocolate muffins
Scrambled eggs with mushrooms
Eggs benedict
Warm potato tortilla with smoked salmon
Baked chèvre
Lobster and fennel salad
Seared scallops with crushed potatoes
Peppered tuna steak with salsa rossa
Pan-fried chicken with creamy beans and leeks
Garlic roasted poussins
Chicken *panini*
Steak with blue cheese butter
Pasta with melted ricotta and herby Parmesan sauce
Gingered chicken noodles
Plum fudge desserts
Fresh figs with vin santo and mascarpone

BEN REED
Sea breeze

FIONA SMITH
Peking-style duck pancake wraps

SONIA STEVENSON
Provençal tian
North African charred vegetables
Traditional fish pie
Coq au vin
Braised lamb shanks with orange and marmalade

FRAN WARDE
Seared tuna salad with lime and soy dressing
Roasted eggplant and Parma ham salad
Chicken liver salad
Roasted salmon wrapped in prosciutto
Korean chicken
Roasted pheasant breasts with bacon, shallots, and mushrooms
Steak and mushroom pie
Chicken and asparagus spaghetti
Couscous with roasted chicken and vegetables
Paella
Potato skins with green dip

LESLEY WATERS
French toast with smoky bacon and spiked tomatoes
Trout fishcakes
Belgian endive, chicory, and radicchio salad with walnut dressing
Seared peppered beef salad with horseradish dressing
Green Thai vegetable curry
Classic creamy mashed potato
Steamed mussels with garlic and vermouth in a foil parcel
Hot wok chile shrimp
Salmon tempura
Seared swordfish with avocado salsa
Saffron fish roast
Mediterranean fish stew
Hot chicken tikka platter with yogurt
Honeyed duck with mango salsa
Gremolata pork with lemon spinach
Venison sausages with port and cranberry ragout
Moroccan lamb tagine
Warm Thai crab rice noodles
Hot whiskey pancakes with raspberries
Luxury hummus

LIGHTNING
BOLT
BOOKS™

The Gateway Arch

Lisa Bullard

Lerner Publications Company
Minneapolis

For Kris,
with love

Lerner Publications Company
A division of Lerner Publishing Group, Inc.
241 First Avenue North
Minneapolis, MN 55401 U.S.A.

Website address: www.lernerbooks.com

Library of Congress Cataloging-in-Publication Data

Bullard, Lisa.
    The Gateway Arch / by Lisa Bullard.
       p.   cm. — (Lightning Bolt Books™—Famous places)
    Includes index.
    ISBN 978-0-8225-9406-2 (lib. bdg. : alk. paper)
    1. Gateway Arch (Saint Louis, Mo.)—Juvenile literature. 2. Arches—Missouri—Saint Louis—Design and construction—Juvenile literature. I. Title.
    TA660.A7B85 2010
    977.8'66—dc22   2008030640

Manufactured in the United States of America
1 2 3 4 5 6 — BP — 15 14 13 12 11 10

Contents

Standing Tall

What is the tallest monument in the United States?

It's the Gateway Arch!
The Gateway Arch is 630
feet (192 meters) tall. It
stands in Saint Louis,
Missouri.

The arch is part of the Jefferson National Expansion Memorial. The Jefferson National Expansion Memorial is a large park. It is named for President Thomas Jefferson.

A history museum is on the park grounds. It stands underneath the Gateway Arch.

When Jefferson was president, he bought lots of land. The United States was able to grow much bigger.

President Thomas Jefferson

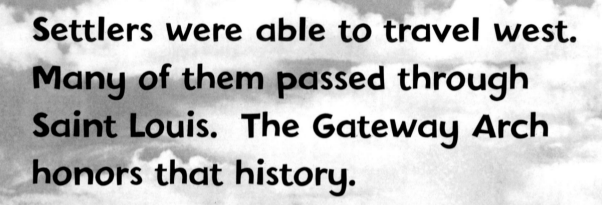

Settlers were able to travel west. Many of them passed through Saint Louis. The Gateway Arch honors that history.

Settlers who wanted to move west often traveled together in wagon trains.

A Slow Start

People first began talking about building a monument to westward growth in 1933. The U.S. government agreed to help pay for it. But plans moved slowly.

People debated about how to pay for the monument.

Planning was put on hold because of World War II (1939–1945).

U.S. soldiers march through Paris, France, during World War II.

A group of citizens held a contest in 1947. They asked architects to compete to create the best design. Eero Saarinen won the contest.

Eero Saarinen created the winning design for the Saint Louis monument.

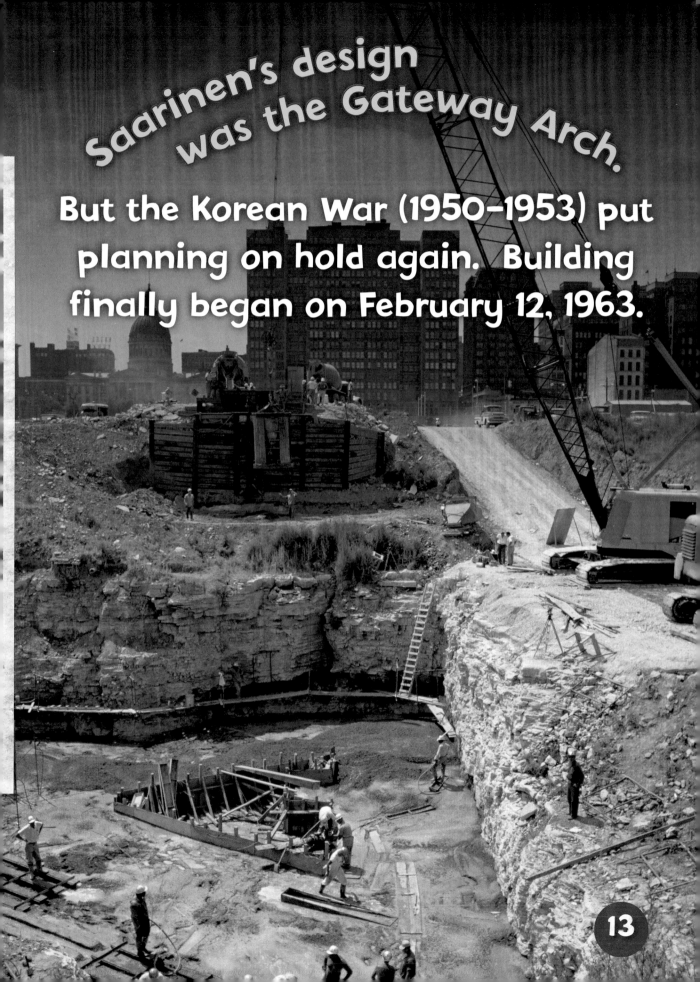

Saarinen's design was the Gateway Arch.

But the Korean War (1950–1953) put planning on hold again. Building finally began on February 12, 1963.

Building the Arch

Each leg of the Gateway Arch has three equal sides. The legs get smaller as they reach higher. At the bottom, each of the three sides is **54** feet (16 m) wide. Each side is **17** feet (5 m) wide at the top.

Visitors to the arch stand near its base. Two sides of the leg can be seen in this photo.

Sunlight reflects off the shiny metal arch.

15

sections shaped like triangles.
Workers used cranes to lift the lower sections.

Workers used cranes to set the first triangular pieces of the arch in place.

Each section was stacked on the one below. Then workers connected them.

New sections were added as the legs grew higher.

Creeper derricks lifted the higher sections. These special machines climbed up the legs on tracks.

18

Workers built both legs of the arch at the same time. It was like building two curving towers. But they had to meet at the top.

This photo of the arch under construction was taken across the Mississippi River from Saint Louis.

Finally, the day came for workers to add the final section. On October 28, 1965, workers slid the last section into place.

Workers move the last section of the arch into place. There are 142 triangular sections that make up the arch.

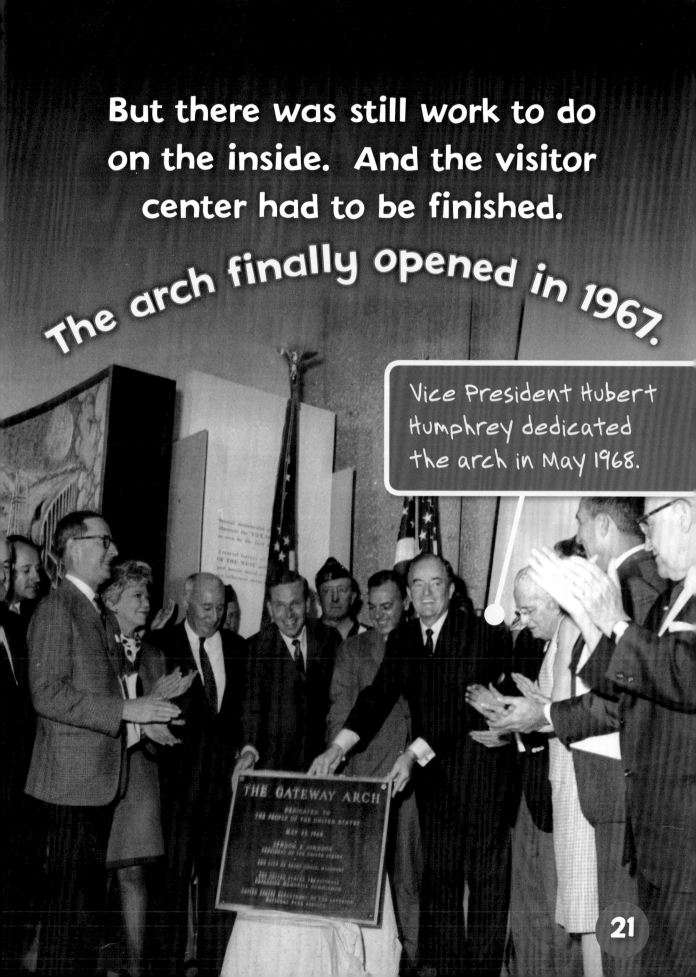

But there was still work to do on the inside. And the visitor center had to be finished.

The arch finally opened in 1967.

Vice President Hubert Humphrey dedicated the arch in May 1968.

THE GATEWAY ARCH

Windows in the observation area (right) give nice views of the city to the west (above).

22

Visiting the Arch

Inside the top of the arch is an observation area. From there, visitors can see up to 30 miles (48 kilometers). But how do people get up there? Regular elevators will not work in the curved legs.

the way to the top. The tram
cars travel inside the legs of
the arch. They move somethi
like Ferris wheel cars. The ride
to the top takes four minutes.

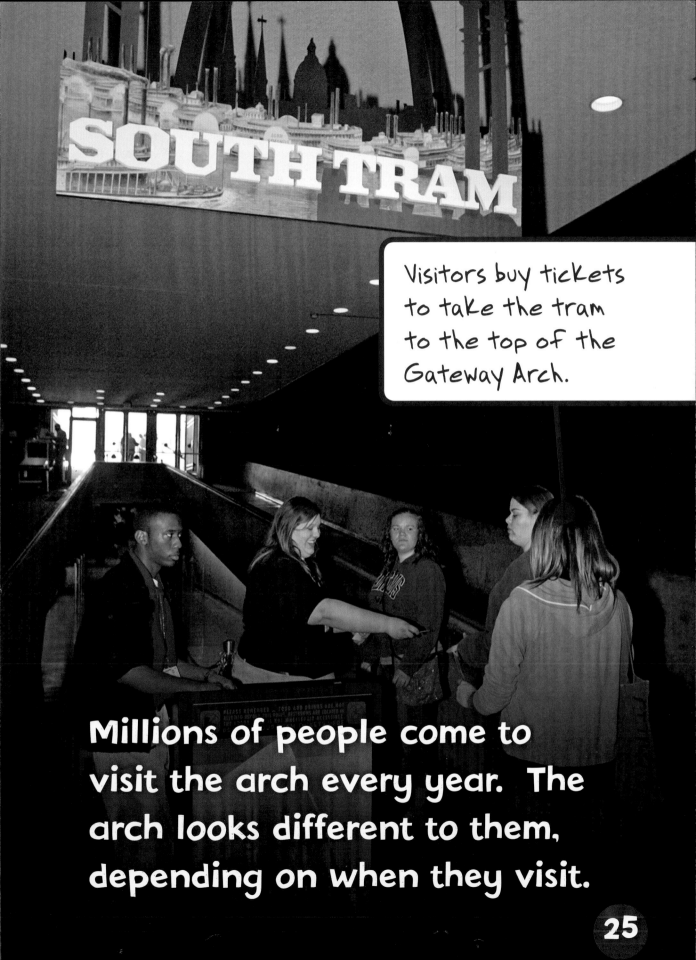

Visitors buy tickets to take the tram to the top of the Gateway Arch.

Millions of people come to visit the arch every year. The arch looks different to them, depending on when they visit.

The arch is reflected in a pool of water.

The look of the arch might change each day. But it reminds every visitor how important Saint Louis was.

It was the gateway to the West.

27

IOWA
Mississippi River
ILLINO
Missouri River
Saint Louis
Miles
0 20 40 60
0 40 80
Kilometers
Jefferson National Expansion Memorial and the Gateway Arch
N
MISSOURI

Fun Facts

- The Gateway Arch is twice as tall as the Statue of Liberty and 75 feet (23 m) taller than the Washington Monument.

- The number 630 is important to the arch. It is 630 feet (192 m) tall. There are 630 feet between the outer edges of the legs.

- The legs of the arch have solid foundations. First, 60-foot (18 m) holes were dug in soil and bedrock. Then they were filled with concrete. More concrete is inside the bottom walls of the legs.

- Architect Eero Saarinen was born in Finland. His family moved to the United States when he was a boy. Sadly, he never got to see the arch built. He died in 1961.

- France once owned a big section of North America. President Thomas Jefferson bought this land in 1803. This was called the Louisiana Purchase.

Glossary

architect: a person who designs buildings

creeper derrick: a lifting machine that can climb tracks up a curved structure such as the arch

design: a plan that shows how something will be built

monument: a statue, building, or other structure that is made to remember a person or event

observation area: a high place where you can see a long distance

stainless steel: a special steel mix that doesn't stain or rust easily

tram: a vehicle you can ride in that is moved by rails and cables

Further Reading

Enchanted Learning: St. Louis Gateway Arch
http://www.enchantedlearning.com/history/us/
monuments/stlouisarch

Gateway Arch Riverfront: Fun Stuff
http://www.gatewayarch.com/Arch/info/arch.fun.aspx

Jefferson National Expansion Memorial
http://www.nps.gov/jeff

Ruffin, Frances E. *The Gateway Arch*. Milwaukee:
Weekly Reader Early Learning Library, 2006.

Sandweiss, Lee Ann. *St. Louis Architecture for Kids*. St.
Louis: Missouri Historical Society Press, 2001.

Schanzer, Rosalyn. *How We Crossed the West: The
Adventures of Lewis and Clark*. Washington, DC:
National Geographic Society, 1997.

Index

Photo Acknowledgments

The images in this book are used with the permission of: © Pete Turner/Iconica/Getty Images, p. 2; © Robert Glusic/Photodisc/Getty Images, pp. 4–5; © Bill Grant/Alamy, p. 6; © Rembrandt Peale/The Bridgeman Art Library/Getty Images, p. 7; © Archive Holdings, Inc./Hulton Archive/Getty Images, p. 8; AP Photo, pp. 9, 19; AP Photo/Peter J. Carroll, pp. 10–11; © Hulton Archive/Getty Images, p. 12; © George F. Mobley/National Geographic/Getty Images, p. 13; © Wesley Hitt/Alamy, p. 14; © Gary Cralle/The Image Bank/Getty Images, p. 15; Jefferson National Expansion Memorial/National Park Service, pp. 16, 17, 18, 20, 21; AP Photo/Tom Gannam, pp. 22, 24, 25; © Ohad Shahar/PhotoStock-Israel/Alamy, p. 23; © Purestock/Getty Images, p. 26; © age fotostock/SuperStock, p. 27; © Laura Westlund/Independent Picture Service, p. 28; © James Blank/Taxi/Getty Images, pp. 30–31.

Front Cover: © Bill Grant/Alamy.